Ernesto Grassi

# THE PRIMORDIAL METAPHOR

translated by Laura Pietropaolo
and Manuela Scarci

# ꟽEDIEVAL & REИAISSAИCE
# TEXTS & STUDIES

VOLUME 121

*The Italian Academy for Advanced Studies in America
is a scholarly research institution located at Casa Italiana
(1161 Amsterdam Avenue, N.Y. 10027) at Columbia University*

Ernesto Grassi

# THE PRIMORDIAL METAPHOR

translated by Laura Pietropaolo
and Manuela Scarci

Medieval & Renaissance texts & studies
in collaboration with the
Italian Academy

Binghamton, New York
1994

**Library of Congress Cataloging-in Publication Data**

Grassi, Ernesto.
    [Metafora inaudita. English]
    The primordial metaphor / Ernesto Grassi ; translated by Laura Pietro-
paolo and Manuela Scarci.
        p.   cm. — (Medieval & Renaissance texts & studies ; v. 121)
    Includes bibliographical references.
    ISBN 0-86698-125-X
        1. Metaphor. 2. Language and languages—Philosophy. 3. Ontology. 4.
Reality. I. Title. II. Series.
    P301.5.M48G7213   1993
    808—dc20                                                        93-43129
                                                                    CIP

This book is made to last.
It is set in Garmond Antiqua,
smythe-sewn and printed on acid-free paper
to library specifications

Printed in the United States of America

# Translators' Note

In preparing this translation of *La metafora inaudita* we have followed the text recently edited by Massimo Marassi (Palermo: Aesthetica Edizioni, 1990). However, we have not adhered completely to it since it contains a few errors, which we have corrected using the typescript supplied to us by the author. The reader is further warned that, given the role of close textual analysis in Grassi's philosophical arguments, we have translated some of the quotations directly from the Italian editions used by the author—or, in a few cases, from the originals themselves—whenever we found the available English versions to be incoherent with his commentary. The Book of Ecclesiastes, for example, could not be quoted from any of the standard English translations without introducing great confusion into Grassi's analysis. As for the special difficulties involved in understanding Grassi in English, we warn the reader that 'abyss' is here the equivalent of the German *Abgrund* understood etymologically as *ab-Grund*, and that 'passion' is always meant etymologically (from the Latin *pati*) as a form of suffering.

# Table of Contents

In desperation
and with the awareness that all is futile
in memory of Elena

And so come to me now
Release me from grievous care
And accomplish what my soul desires
And be my ally

Sappho, *Hymn to Aphrodite*

# Preface to the English Edition

The title of this work may appear strange. In fact, what is primordial remains unheard; it is not self-evident from the beginning, nor do we know how it manifests itself to us. The chapters follow one another and comprise a single unit like the parts of a story which will be revealed in its entirety only at the end, and even then its completeness and its perfection will remain concealed to us. The theme will emerge gradually even in those places, such as the first chapters, where it will not be fully comprehensible to us in a first reading. As we shall see, authors and texts so different from each other with respect to time and historical perspective, to content and field of interest, will come together revealing the double weave of a complex tapestry. We are thus invited to read the world and history simultaneously. Reality can become apparent to us in its constitutive duality only if we guarantee for it a correct interpretation. The criterion, the principle which regulates the naturalness of such a coming to presence is metaphor. But this metaphor is certainly not the metaphor that is intended as a rhetorical figure, the mere transposition of meaning from one thing to another. On the contrary, since the meaning of things is ontologically a trope of the being which constitutes them, metaphor is nothing other than the modality through which what is 'originary' is revealed to us and by means of which words carry the appeal of the abyss. Metaphor is therefore a continuous task and an uncontrollable possibility. Can it be that in this way, despite its infinite valences, we reach the ultimate word, the word which bespeaks the diverse meanings of beings while pointing to the only root they have in common? The analysis of the authors we have tried to interpret speaks well to the contrary. Metaphor, as the language of that which is originary, remains, despite our uninterrupted quest, a word which is unspoken and therefore unheard, but is also, for this very reason, irrepressibly marvelous and disturbing. We were looking for an 'exquisite' word, a 'sublime' word, a word which would provide us with a definitive answer to all of our questions, a word in which truth, in all of its roundness, would loom bright as the ultimate point of arrival at the end of our quest. But the word, well before we began to wonder about it, to question it, has emerged for us, not as a definitive entity, but as a suggestion passing from utterance to utterance, as if to hint that this never-ending process carries the meaning of our own wondering and of the wondering of the word itself. And so we reach an impasse as we stop before the word, which refuses to show its countenance to us. We would like some 'exquisite' word to offer itself to us in revelation. But since this 'lost' word eludes us, we trust that the sacred will yet speak to us, perhaps more discretely, more softly, in the echo of a whisper.

In this sense, the book's dedication is no mere poetic reference; it documents, rather, the motivation, the direction, and the goal of our quest.

I would like to thank Rita Rebel and Enrichetta Valenziani for having transcribed my notes. Finally, my heartfelt gratitude goes to my friend Massimo Marassi for his invaluable help in the redaction of this work.

Munich, Fall 1988.

# Metaphor as an Element of Originary Language

## 1) The Problem

The process of speaking rationally constitutes a legitimation of our statements, and all teaching based on the choice of such method consists in giving, clarifying, and explaining 'reasons.' In teaching, the teacher points them out. In so doing, however, all pedagogical activity is reduced to the transference of something known only to the instructor: it is a monologue, not a dialogue. Knowledge, which marks Western culture, has differed clearly, ever since its origins, from mere opinion (*dóxa*): what we have an opinion about can surely be true, but it is different from what we know, in so far as opinion is not backed by reasons.

In the *Meno*, Plato uses an interesting metaphor to explain this difference: He compares opinion to a slave who, if not chained, can always escape. The 'chain' anchors assertions to reason.[1] Knowledge, understood as a rational process, implies the exclusion of all uncertainty about the subject matter to which we anchor our statements. The basis of knowledge acquires, therefore, a normative, controlling character: only grounded knowledge can be considered valid. For this reason the Greeks called the principles on which knowledge is grounded the *archai* (in fact, *archein* means to rule, to be in charge, and the *archontes* were those who ruled, those who were in charge).

The *archai* we are referring to must be valid anywhere at any

---

[1] *Meno*, 97d–98a.

time, and the language which expresses this way of thinking must be logical and rational. Consequently, any kind of poetic, imaginative, rhetorical language, namely language limited to a specific time and place, must be excluded from the sphere of theoretical or scientific thought. In this sphere it cannot claim any rights. But we must not forget that modern analytic philosophy and logical positivism deny metaphysics the ability to create scientific thought. The validity of the rational process is limited to the sphere marked by the principles and axioms on which science has laid its foundations. In turn, such principles and axioms cannot, of themselves, be scientific, since, by definition, they cannot be proven: to justify them by resorting to some original evidence or intuition would open the door to arbitrariness. Consequently, any humanism that attempts to transcend formal thinking by taking into consideration the problems of life and man must be excluded, and with it must be rejected any 'pathetic' elements inherent in poetic or rhetorical language. Rational and scientific language must necessarily leave out of its scope the passions[2] of man. Its ideal is a mathematical one and the link between the human world and rationality generates the terror of falling into subjectivism and arbitrariness.

## 2) The 'E' at Delphi

How does classical antiquity view the problem of the indemonstrability of principles and, therefore, of their archaic character? In order to clarify the terms of the problem, I shall turn to Plutarch's treatise *On the 'E' at Delphi*. The treatise tells of a sacred offer made to Apollo.[3] The Delphic coins carrying the image of the Emperor Hadrian (AD 117–138) show a frontal view of the great temple of Apollo at Delphi. Between two central columns, high on the coin, hangs the striking capital letter 'E'. What is its meaning? To understand the discussion about it recorded in the treatise we must keep in mind that in ancient writing, still adhered to in fifth-century inscriptions, the letter *epsilon* (e) can signify either the conjunction 'if' or the verbal form 'you are.'

---

[2] The reader is warned that "passion" and its derivatives are always meant etymologically (from the Latin *pati*) as a form of suffering (translators' note).

[3] Text and English translation by F. C. Babbit in *Plutarch's Moralia*, vol. 5 (Cambridge, MA: Harvard Univ. Press, 1936), 193–253.

Long before Plutarch wrote his treatise in the form of a dialogue, the meaning of the symbol had become the object of several hypotheses. Plutarch reviews them all. The first hypothesis, proposed in the text by Plutarch's brother Lamprias, states that 'E' is simply the fifth letter of the alphabet and that, as such, it is the graphic representation of the number 5. Placed on the pediment of the temple of Apollo, it signifies that the god is witness to the belief that the true original sages of Greece were five in number (Chilon, Thales, Solon, Bias and Pittacus). This thesis can be described as historical.

In the second interpretation, 'E' is the second vowel of the Greek alphabet and, according to Plutarch's text, symbolizes the sun, the second planet, equivalent in essence to Apollo, the Lord of Delphi, the very light of Wisdom. This interpretation is astronomical in nature.

In the third interpretation, 'E' stands for 'if,' as in "if only the heavens ...," namely, the beginning of the formulaic official prayer with which at Delphi one would address Apollo: "Oh, if only our god ... etc." This is an essentially sacred interpretation.

The fourth interpretation is the one which calls our attention. Its advocate Theon states that 'E' is the linguistic particle expressing the conditional function 'if' which indicates the basis and point of departure of every rational judgement: if we posit a premise, we must draw from it a specific conclusion. The linguistic particle, therefore, takes on the connotations of a warning: whoever makes a pilgrimage to Delphi is committed to rational thinking and thus honors Apollo, god of rationality. This is a philosophical interpretation. The passage of interest to us is the following:

> And since philosophy is directed at truth, since the light of truth is proof, and sentence structure the origin of proof, it is understandably the word that creates and achieves this connection which wise men dedicate to the god who loves truth above all. The god is a seer, and the faculty of seeing is that faculty which points from the present or past into the future: nothing is created without a cause and nothing is seen without a reason. ...[4]

Moreover, Plutarch states further on: "Therefore, though it may be risky to say this, I shall not omit to say that the tripod of truth is

---

[4] 387 a–b.

reason itself, which first draws the conclusion from the premiss, then proceeds to the existence of the thing, and thence to the completion of the proof."[5] This text contains the most radical rationalization, and the most radical demythologization not only of philosophical thought, but also of the faculty of foresight, originally attributed to divine beings. Here philosophy is identified solely with the rational ability of reaching conclusions, of providing proof and of 'fore-see-ing'; consequently, prophecy is the result of a purely rational process.

Plutarch's treatise deserves further consideration because the entire argument, despite its rational nature, is enveloped from the very beginning in the aura of the sacred, of the divine. The god helps his beseechers as the originary force which arouses and assists those who address questions to him. But how? Plutarch provides the following answer:

> Since ... inquiry is the beginning of philosophy, and wonder and uncertainty the beginning of inquiry, it seems only natural that the greater part of what concerns the god should be concealed in riddles, and should call for some account of the wherefore and an explanation of its cause. [6]

## 3) The Problem of Wonder

Why is the sense of wonder, as the origin of inquiry, of primary importance to the essence of philosophy? Why is a sacred significance attributed to this sense of wonder?

Both Plato and Aristotle relate the phenomenon of wonder (*thaumazein*) to the origin of philosophy. In the *Theatetus*, Socrates argues that philosophy originates from wonder and states that "he was a good genealogist who made Iris the daughter of Thaumas."[7] Aristotle describes the relation between wonder and the origin of philosophy and says that "it is owing to their wonder that men both now begin and at first began to philosophize."[8]

---

[5] 387 c.

[6] 385 c.

[7] *Theaetetus*, 155 d. English translation by F. M. Cornford in Plato, *The Collected Dialogues*, ed. E. Hamilton and H. Cairns (Princeton, NJ: Princeton Univ. Press, 1961).

[8] *Metaphysics* 982 b 12. English translation by W. D. Ross in *The Complete*

The grammarian and lexicographer Hesychius gives in his lexicon the following synonyms for *thauma*: *ekplexis* (shock); *xenisma* (estrangement); and for *thaumazein*: *theasthai* (to look) and *manthanein* (to learn, to understand).[9] A later etymological definition also derives *thaumazein* from *theasthai*.[10] The etymological connection established both in antiquity and in modern times between *thaumazo* and *theaomai* points to the area in which the interpretation of the term *thaumazein* is to be looked for: on the one hand in 'seeing,' and on the other in the domain of 'immediacy,' which establishes the relationship between 'wonder' and 'emerging vision,' already present in the prephilosophical use of the term *thaumazein*.[11]

Perhaps the connection we have emphasized between seeing and wondering is best expressed in the genealogy of the goddess Iris, who is introduced in the passage I have already quoted from Plato's *Theaetetus* as the personification of the wonder of philosophy. In this genealogy we find the elements already contained in the etymological allusions: estrangement and the questions it engenders. Iris is the daughter of Thaumas, who, as the son of Gaea, creator of all things in heaven and on earth, is directly associated with the beginning of all existence, which, as the originary and non-deducible being, fills with wonder. Iris is the personification of the rainbow, which joins heaven and earth, above and below, everything visible. As the daughter of Thaumas, Iris presides over the relationships between gods and men and is the winged messenger and the giver of the word, according to the etymology of her name deriving from *erein*, 'to say,' 'to speak.' Moreover, according to Alcaeus, the union of Iris with the rain god Zephyrus produced Eros, the god of love, who answers every question and satisfies every impulse.[12]

The relation between wonder and the need to question emerges

---

*Works of Aristotle,* the revised Oxford translation, ed. J. Barnes (Princeton, NJ: Princeton Univ. Press, 1984).

[9] *Hesychii Alexandrini Lexicon,* ed. K. Latle (Hauniae: Ejnar Munksgaard, 1966), 2:308.

[10] H. Frisk, *Griechisches etymologisches Wörterbuch,* ed. H. Frisk (Heidelberg: 1960), 1:656.

[11] Homer, *Iliad* 18, 467 ff.; *Odyssey* 3, 373; 7, 145; 10, 326.

[12] Alcaeus, fr. 13 in *Poetae Lyrici Graeci,* ed. T. Bergk (Leipzig: 1882), vol. 3; fr. 8 in *Anthologica Lyrica,* vol. 4, *Poetae Melici,* ed. H. Diehl (Leipzig: 1923).

only if something presents itself to us as a problem: no one, in fact, will question what is unequivocal. It is rather what 'concerns us,' what awakens our interest, that becomes the object of a question. Questions arise only when something demands clarification, because uncertainty would be intolerable. In other words, we must find ourselves in the realm of an originary tension for our 'at-tention' to be awakened. That is why the estrangement referred to by Hesychius in his lexicon is related to shock.

## 4) *Philosophical* Pistis

We must now ask ourselves the following question: Can we find in the Greek philosophical tradition a continuing presence of this issue which can provide us with the foundation for our thesis on the origin of metaphoric, historical language?

In his *Metaphysics* Aristotle makes a statement of capital importance:

> For those who wish to get clear of difficulties it is advantageous to state the difficulties well; for the subsequent free play of thought implies the solution of the previous difficulties, and it is not possible to untie a knot which one does not know [...]. Therefore one should have surveyed all the difficulties beforehand [...] because people who inquire without first stating the difficulties are like those who do not know where they have to go.[13]

In order to understand the significance of this passage, we must stress the pre-eminence of metaphoric language *vis-à-vis* logical language. First of all, Aristotle, in the cited passage, uses a metaphor: "it is not possible to untie a knot of which one does not know." This metaphor points out that the feeling of nonindifference before a problem is concretely experienced when one is 'tied' in a 'knot' to an objectivity from which he cannot free himself. Only by going back to it will he be able to recognize his ignorance, a fact which constitutes the first step towards knowledge as well as the way to dispel the state of uncertainty in which he finds himself.

The objectivity of the source, of that which is 'originary,' mani-

---

[13] Metaphysics 995 a 27–37.

fests itself concretely as the responsibility of taking on a task that must be accomplished. Such urgency appears primarily as a sense of wonder. It is immediate (un-mediated) and therefore it is indicative rather than demonstrative. Consequently, it awakens the need to ask questions so that we may unveil the meaning of phenomena by freeing an 'originary vision' (*theasthai*) of them. Moreover, wonder has a pathetic nature: *pathos*, the emotion accompanying wonder, is the expression of our experience of being compelled to seek an explanation.

Since the phenomenon of wonder occurs within the realm of what is originary, of what is not deducible, the *thaumazein* is the expression of the experience of astonishment and estrangement. This is why the originary manifests itself only instantaneously and directly with all the characteristics of a compelling force and of an urgent need in the here and now of existence. It manifests itself in human history and is not logically deducible. It is exclusively in this realm that man experiences wonder as the origin of knowledge. It is also in this experience that we find the source of the meaning of the mysterious 'e' at Delphi, and not in Plutarch's rational interpretation of it.

Now, where can we find legitimation for our interpretation of the origin of knowledge, as conceived by Aristotle—to whom we traditionally attribute the notion of the pre-eminence of rational thought and language? Aristotle's position with respect to the structure and the archaic status of principles must be included in our discussion of the problem of *arché*, of the manifestation of the meaning of individual beings and of the nonrational structure of language. Aristotle maintains that "not to know of what things one may demand demonstration, and of what one may not, argues simply want of education."[14] In his *Posterior Analytics*, he insists on this point using the term *pistis* (conviction, belief), a term of fundamental importance in the history of Western thought. He states:

> Hence if we know and are convinced because of the primitives, we both know and are convinced of them better, since it is because of them that we know and are convinced of what is posterior.[15]

---

[14] *Metaphysics* 1006 a 5.
[15] *Analytica Posteriora* 72 a 30ff. English translation by J. Barnes in *The Complete Works of Aristotle*.

The Christian tradition has attributed a religious significance to the word *pistis*. In the Aristotelian passage, however, the term is found in relation to the analysis of the structure of principles, of the *archai*. If scientific knowledge is born of the persuasion grounded in demonstration, it follows that he who has attained knowledge by virtue of such demonstration (persuasion) must necessarily possess an even firmer conviction (*pistis*) of the principles on which it is grounded.[16] What does *pistis* mean here? It cannot be understood as a renunciation of knowledge—a dogmatic faith—nor can it be reduced to opinion (*dóxa*). What constitutes then the structure of originary knowledge which governs the world of human knowledge?

To answer such a question we must go back to the founding principle of Aristotelian logic and see how it should be interpreted. The principle of noncontradiction is considered by Aristotle the basic principle of thinking and speaking: "The same attribute cannot at the same time belong and not belong to the same object and in the same respect."[17]

We can interpret correctly the Aristotelian statement only if we take into consideration the way in which Aristotle demonstrates his axiom. But by asking such a question, are we not risking contradiction, right from the start? It is obvious that the principle of a demonstration, given its *archaic* status, cannot be logically proven, because it is itself the very foundation of logic. Aristotle, in fact, does not offer a logical, rational proof but a proof he calls 'elenctic'. What is its structure?

The Greek verb *elegchein* means, among other things, 'to tie to the pillory'; whoever is tied in such a manner is 'exposed' to eventual derision. The elenctic demonstration is radically different from a rational one because it does not resort to reason for its own legitimation; it resorts rather to the indication of an undeniable connection. In fact, whoever denies the principle of contradiction, if he wishes to say something that has meaning, must necessarily make use of it. He must acknowledge its dominion.[18] To exist is to be 'tied' to the need for the significant word.

---

[16] *Analytica Posteriora* 72 a 35.

[17] *Metaphysics* 1005 b 19.

[18] *Metaphysics* 1006 a 20.

Even if he were to have recourse to silence—so as not to be obliged to contradict himself—his silence would be a meaningful statement as well. Man is chained to the pillory of the word. He must speak: his very silence is a sign of this.

Is this our Promethean fate? In depicting the lament of Prometheus who, chained to the solitude of the rock, is exposed to the derision of the day and the darkness of the night, Aeschylus has him exclaim: "Under such suffering, speech and silence are alike beyond me."[19]

*Pistis* is neither opinion, nor rational knowledge. Nor is it a dogmatic conviction related to a religious revelation. The elenctic nature of the principle of contradiction compels us to acknowledge the presence of suffering, of endurance, which testifies to the impossibility of an escape from meaning. *Pistis* must be here understood as the result of a fundamental experience, of a task which implies at once the signal of a question and the need for an answer. In the context of such experience, the temporal and spatial significance of beings manifests itself each time in accordance with the urgency of the here and now. Thus man finds himself called upon to respond to his passionate need to speak and to question.

Since being is present in all statements relative to individual beings—i.e., participles or entities participating in being (in fact, we say that every being exists, is)—the original need to respond to its calling expresses itself in an appropriate verbal form. But what verbal form does it assume? It does not take on a logical, deductive form; it assumes, rather, an indicative metaphorical one, by virtue of which every expression *is itself* and, at the same time, is not itself since it is only the response to the call of being, which asserts itself in the here and now of existence. It is not an abstract word, dissociated from time and space; it is rather a historical, rhetorical word.

We can therefore draw a conclusion which is essential to the formulation of our problem: Rational thought no longer represents the originary approach to the understanding of the being of beings. In such a context being is enveloped in contradiction, in the abyss[20] of what is rationally undefinable. But, from a different perspective, the

---

[19] Aeschylus, *Prometheus Bound*, 105–106. English translation by P. Vellacott (Penguin Books, 1961).

[20] The reader is warned that "abyss" is here the equivalent of the German *Abgrund* understood etymologically as *ab-Grund* (translators' note).

undefinable fills us with wonder. Wonder moves us and turns us away from a nonhistorical consideration of beings.

## 5) Metaphor as the Root of Knowledge: Coluccio Salutati.

Is there a tradition which offers a foundation for a conception of knowledge rooted in the historicity of ontological experience? Does the humanist tradition offer us such a possibility? A correct understanding of Humanism has been hindered by the pre-eminence of German idealism, which denied it any philosophical value precisely because it is grounded on rhetorical and metaphorical thought; by Heidegger's antihumanistic thesis; and by the interpretation of Humanism as essentially a Christian reflection on Platonism.

With regard to the concept of knowledge, Western philosophy rejected, from the very beginning, the speculative function of rhetorical language for its being anchored to the here and now of existence; consequently, it expressed a negative judgement on metaphor, since metaphor transfers and transforms the meaning of a word and, in so doing, destroys its rational precision.

We would like to propose a different thesis: That which is—namely, individual beings, participants in and participles of being, for only as such do they exist—manifests itself in reality exclusively in a concrete historical situation, defined by the here and now of existence. All beings, in their openness to being, are expressions of a call, an appeal that must be answered in the urgency of every moment. The appeals, in whose realm we exist, are everchanging and new, and the meaning of beings is transformed according to the modality of our responses to the appeals.

We shall reformulate our question: Is there a tradition which allows us to identify a nonrational foundation of knowledge, by virtue of which metaphor and rhetorical language acquire a philosophical function? I have tried elsewhere[21] to reconstruct this tradition and here I shall summarize it with references to *De Laboribus Herculis* by Coluccio Salutati (1331-1406).[22]

---

[21] E. Grassi, *Renaissance Humanism: Studies in Philosophy and Poetics*, Medieval and Renaissance Texts and Studies, vol. 51 (Binghamton, NY, 1988).

[22] Coluccio Salutati, *De Laboribus Herculis*, ed. B.L. Ullman (Zurich: Thesauri Mundi, 1951).

Salutati states that *scientia* originates in a metaphorical activity which consists of the discovery, of the 'invention' (from *inventio* meaning 'to find') of *similitudines* which identify on each occasion the everchanging differing meaning of beings. In order to understand his thesis we must begin with the analysis of the arguments and of the terminology he used in this text, which differ immensely from those of traditional metaphysics. Salutati maintains that *scientia* has its origins in the Muses, not in just one of them, but in the common activity of all nine. Only the Muses make possible the search for knowledge, *scientiam quaerere*,[23] and the achievement of *doctrina perfecta*.[24] We shall limit our analysis to the interpretation of the first six Muses.

First of all, Salutati indicates the method and the point of departure for the scholar. Strikingly, this method (*meta odou*) does not constitute a rational, pedagogical set of directions, but is rather a response to three existential impulses. The scholar must heed the impulse to Glory; he must feel desperately and passionately the desire to attain knowledge. Salutati identifies this impulse with the first of the Muses, Clio: *Prima namque cogitationi discere cupientium primum occurrit fame celebritas que Gloria est.*[25] We are clearly nowhere near any rational presupposition as far as the method is concerned.

The second originary impulse we must respond to is the impulse to pleasure (*edoné*). Again it is a passion, it is the pleasure in learning personified by another muse, Euterpe: *Alteram vero ponit Euterpen, quod Latine dicit nihil aliud esse quam 'bene delectans'.*[26]

The third presupposition behind the quest for knowledge is represented by Melpomene: *Tertiam autem Melpomenem statuit, hoc est, inquit, 'Meditationem faciens permancre'.*[27] Perseverance in study is also necessary: it is not a passion, but an attitude (*exis*).

Therefore, the path to follow in our search for knowledge is characterized by a threefold commitment.

After having made these considerations on method, how does Salutati identify the other constitutive elements of knowledge? They

---

[23] Salutati, I, 9, 11.
[24] Salutati, I, 9, 14.
[25] Salutati, I, 9, 10.
[26] Salutati, I, 9, 11.
[27] Salutati, I, 9, 12.

are defined in relation to three nonrational activities. The first is sensory *perceptio*, the passion of the senses, the passionate experience of what manifests itself through the sensory organs and constitutes the premise of every search. This is the world of phenomena, of all that appears (*phainomenon, phaineshai*). This passion of the senses, again represented by a muse, is seen by Salutati as the faculty of perception which produces the germs of knowledge: *Sequentem autem Taliam locavit in ordine, quam 'capacitatem' vult sive 'germina ponentem'.*[28]

Let us keep in mind that phenomena, all that appears, do not acquire meaning in an abstract manner, of themselves; their meaning is determined by that of which the senses, in so far as they are organs, are the instruments.

Organs of what, then? Certainly of a passion in every way originary, nondeducible, the passion of a Muse, as Salutati calls it. We are dealing with a passionate experience linked to an *originary reality*, which compellingly asserts itself in and through its instruments, the sensory organs. It is therefore an indicative, not a demonstrative passion, and as such it is nondeducible and must be recognized as a force arising from the mystery of the abyss. Consequently, Salutati defines it as the expression of a Muse, thus advancing a thesis essentially antithetical to traditional metaphysics, whose point of departure is the problem of individual beings and their logical definition. Salutati grounds his thesis on the passion of the appeal of the abyss within which the meaning of every being emerges.

Salutati, however, points out that mere perception—the submersion of oneself in the ocean of perceptible phenomena—is not sufficient to acquire knowledge, *doctrina, scientia*. Two other human faculties are necessary. The first is memory, because we need to remember the *perceptum*, that which has been revealed by the sensory organs: *...parum est didicisse nisi commemores iam percepta, quintam Polimiam enumerat quasi 'multa memorantem'.*[29] Memory is represented by Polyhymnia, the Muse whose name, according to Salutati, signifies the ability to remember many things. What is being proposed is a form of remembering as *ri-cor-dare*, that is to say a return to the heart of the matter, or to its being.

---

[28] Ibid.
[29] Ibid.

But as Salutati observes—we limit ourselves to perceiving and remembering the essence of that which is manifest, if we halt before the phenomena, all our efforts to acquire *scientia* are futile. In fact, he who does not make the effort to find similarity among things is not yet a learned man: *Verum adhuc doctus non est qui ex his que perceperit nescit in similium inventionem erumpere.*[30] Erato is the Muse who presides over the finding of similarities (*similia inveniens*), who presides over knowledge and allows for the passage from the similar to the similar (*de similibus in similia se trasferre*).[31] Therefore, for those who wish to discover the essence of *scientia*, Erato's activity, which follows perception and memory, is absolutely decisive.

What is the meaning of finding, of discovering the *similitudo*? It is to provide the premise for the transfer of meanings, to discern the origin of *metapherein*, the very essence of poetic language. Thus, knowledge is grounded on metaphoric language, which pertains to the realm of poetry.

Salutati repeatedly stresses the 'fascinating' effect of poetry, which depends on the fact that poetic language is metaphorical or transferred. The language of the poets separates men from that which the senses make manifest (*adeo revocavit a sensibus*) so that they believe in something completely different from that which they have perceived through their eyes (*quod ipsos id fecerit opinari cuius contrarium visibiliter percepissent*).[32]

What exactly triggers for Salutati the perception of *similitudines*, the perception of what different beings have in common? It is *ingenium*. It is the poet who reveals the historicity of our world (*ingenii altitudine*).[33]

Incidentally, in Salutati's thesis we find expressed what Vico, three centuries later, would consider the essence of the humanist tradition.

At this point we must ask ourselves what does the stimulus to learn consist of and in the realm of what type of experience does knowledge disclose itself? On the basis of our discussion, we must point out that only in passionate experience can we find a sign of the

---

[30] Ibid.
[31] Ibid.
[32] Salutati, I, 1, 18.
[33] Salutati, II, *prima editio. Liber primus*, 587.

appeal of being addressed to all that becomes manifest. *Scientia* originates in the urgency of compelling, concrete questions: problems originate from man's historicity, in the situation determined by them. In this sense, the humanist tradition must be lauded for having cultivated philology in view of the understanding of our historical tradition. Humanist education has provided the image of man developing and shaping himself through the study of the meaning of words forever changing in accordance with the historical perspective within which words must be experienced. Now, to return to our initial statement regarding an ideal for teaching, we can reaffirm that such an ideal does not consist in the knowledge imparted by the teacher, nor is it a mere mnemonic exercise on the part of the student. Teaching must be based on a sense of wonder, or the emotion awakened by the text to be studied. It is a wonder which is nurtured by experiencing the changes of the meaning of the words in the act of interpretation. Only in this way can we be filled with wonder before the ingenious, inventive activity of writers who try to respond in various historical situations, to the different appeals of originary reality. Each work becomes thus a metaphor of the urgent appeal of originary reality, which we can identify only through the passionate experience of the Muse, characteristic of an essentially humanist tradition, and not by virtue of the *ratio*.

# The Underivedness of the Spoken Word
## *Phoné* as an Element of Language

### 1) Sound and the Spoken Word

In one of his autobiographical works, *My Universities*, Maxim Gorky recalls a question which was posed to him by a peasant: " 'Can't you explain it to me, brother? How it comes about? Here a man looks at these little crooks and curlicues, and they turn into words, and—I know those words! Our own words, that we're always using! [They are alive and ours] But how do I know them? There is nobody whispering them in my ear. If it was pictures—well, then I could understand. But this way—it's like as if I saw somebody's very thoughts, printed right here on the page. How can it be?' What answer could I give him? And he was grieved by my 'I don't know.' "[1]

We can ask the very same question about *language*: it is made up of spoken words (*phonai*) which, in turn, are made up of sounds (*psophoi*); these give rise to words which, as Gorky says, are 'alive' and 'ours.' Why do we recognize their meaning? Does someone tell us their meaning? Obviously not. Then how does this metaphor of sounds occur? How are meanings 'transferred' into sounds so that these become words? In an attempt to answer this question, I shall follow a method opposite to the one followed by traditional rhetoric: I shall start by stating the conclusions I have reached and later expound the reasoning which has led me to them.

---

[1] M. Gorky, *Autobiography, My Universities*, ed. A. Yarmolinsky (New York: Collier, 1962), 597.

Let us bear in mind the first lines of *Perí Hermeneias* by Aristotle: "Spoken sounds (*phoné*) are symbols of affections in the soul."[2] The point of departure of Western metaphysics is the problem of beings, their meaning; the metaphysical tradition attempts to define the being of beings through the rational process. It seems to be a perfectly legitimate method of proceeding, since beings—as the word itself suggests—are 'participles' of and participate in being. On the other hand, the explanation of the being of beings can take place only through a logical process which, by appealing to some valid reasons, claims to reach objectivity.

That logical process is essentially an abstract one; it disregards the here and now seen as relative elements and thus reaches a universal which is considered valid anywhere anytime. To transfer a meaning to a sound by means of a rational process is, for example, the method Plato adopted to introduce Socrates; such a method was deemed necessary to refute the subjective relativistic theses of the Sophists. However, we ask ourselves: Is this traditional pattern of philosophy, which was decisive for Western thought, still valid today?

The logical process, by means of logical definitions, programmatically *abstracts* the here and now of beings, while we, in fact, passionately experience them in concrete situations. To abstract from these, and to claim to have thereby come to apprehend the being of beings, implies the use of thoughts and words which are completely abstract, of those very thoughts and words which belong precisely to traditional logic and metaphysics.

But we must ask ourselves: Where do beings first manifest themselves? Through the senses, within the limits of pleasure and pain, in original sensations which, in turn, are the origin of every passion, such as the fear of proving incapable of identifying the meaning of phenomena, the hope of succeeding in this task, the envy of those who do succeed in it, the goodwill and the desire to take part in their work in order to share in their friendship and love. Let us keep in mind that what manifests itself (*phainomenon*) appears through organs, that is through the instruments which are the senses. The

---

[2] *De interpretatione*, 16 a 4; English translation by J. L. Ackrill in *The Complete Works of Aristotle*, the revised Oxford translation, ed. J. Barnes (Princeton, NJ: Princeton Univ. Press, 1984).

problem of assigning meaning to what we perceive through the senses can only be solved if we know the code which discloses the meaning of what appears, a code whose instruments are precisely the senses.

I have spoken of 'code,' a term which today is ambiguous, and I would not want to be misunderstood. Semioticians use the term in a subjective manner, as synonymous with a key individually chosen to decipher and, therefore, apprehend the signs of reality; that choice, seen as deliberate, helps to disclose and read the meaning of beings. The code of the senses, of which I speak, however, *is not subjective*, nor is it chosen arbitrarily. It is, instead, passionately experienced and endured by the senses. What they reveal to us appears in the realm of pleasure and pain: these are the characteristics with which the meaning of *phainomena*, of perceptible appearances, originally prevailed. In this case, there is no duality of code and reality to decode; there is only the immediate appearance of indicative sensory data in the passions we endure. Since all that appears manifests itself within the limits of pleasure (*edonê*) and pain (*lype*), the respective phenomena have a passionate character because the code of the senses, which illustrates and reveals, urges and presses from within, and is endured by all.

In the *De anima* Aristotle insisted that the fundamental element of language (*logos*), the spoken word that is, "is a meaningful sound."[3] We are therefore compelled to conclude that spoken words, too, have a passionate character, since they appear within the limits of pleasure and pain, as signs indicative of how and to what extent the needs, whose organs or instruments are the senses, are met. But what exactly are they indicative of?

Aristotle basically distinguished sounds from the spoken words— we shall see later how, in doing so, he predetermined the fate of traditional metaphysics—and later defined the spoken word as an indicative sign (*psophos semantikós*). From that we are supposed to infer not only that the spoken word constitutes something completely new with respect to sound, but that the spoken word is a metaphor which originates from the transference (*metapherein*) of meaning, of an indicative sign, to sound (*sema*). Was Aristotle then refuting the thesis which maintains the primariness and nondeducibility of an original,

---

[3] *On the Soul* 420 b 30; English translation by J. A. Smith in *The Complete Works of Aristotle.*

mysterious, groundless horizon that is dependent upon a code for its disclosure? Was Aristotle not maintaining only the duality of a code for beings which are to be interpreted in light of that code?

Conceiving the code in such a manner presupposes not only—to say it in modern terms—the duality of subject and object, but also the presence of a *rational process*, a *causal process* (a cause and effect which reveal the code), and a *temporal process* (a before and after) on which the emergence of our world depends. Thus the problem of 'why' becomes dominant above all others: we ask for explanations and explore the problem of the truth of beings in relation to the problem of an original manifestation pointing to the being of beings. But what are the arguments Aristotle turned to in order to demonstrate such a thesis? The thesis is—as we shall presently see—mechanical in nature; it depends on a causal process since it refers to the succession of cause and effect. But can we explain the emergence of the spoken word, of the semantic indicative sign through this process? Every causal explanation leaves out of consideration, abstracts from the fundamental given fact that sound manifests itself exclusively through an organ, an instrument functioning because of a call which, in its mysterious nature, needs to be answered. The rational mechanical explanation does not take into consideration the fact that sound depends on an instrument for its manifestation: the sense organ, an instrument which always refers back to what it is the instrument of, to what we can never lose sight of, if we want to understand its meaning. A sound which does not appear for the organ of hearing does not exist; it is mechanical, causal, and technical: a pure abstraction.

Precisely because everything that manifests itself through the senses appears within the limits of pleasure and pain, it always achieves, in view of these limits, its passionate indicative meaning of origin. We must then infer that there are no sounds, no tastes, no smells, no colors without meaning, but that there are, instead, always and only meaningful sensible 'phenomena'. The world which manifests itself through the senses is our world of origin; it is the senses which raise the curtain of the theater whose stage we enter both as actors and, at the same time, as spectators. The indicative semantic voice arises through pleasure and pain, from the depths of a groundless original reality, as an instantaneous nondeducible manifestation, without distinction between cause and effect, without a before and after, without a reason. Such is the profound meaning of the relentless defense of pleasure attempted by Lorenzo Valla in the *De volup-tate*. But do the preceding considerations succeed in justifying the thesis of the metaphorical nature of language as constituted by mean-ingful sounds? What is the point of speaking of metaphor? All that appears through the senses proves to be an expression of continuous suffering, of an identifiable and yet unidentifiable call, something which appears and goes beyond the individual being manifesting itself. We find ourselves before a primary event, before the coming about of the orderly world, of the sensible *kosmos*.

If we are compelled to recognize this given primary fact, this presentiveness, this instantaneous event—that is *in-stans* as *hic-stare*—philosophy today can discover a new sense for itself if its point of departure becomes the passionate nature of sensible phenomena. In fact, we must admit decidedly that for us there are no phenomena abstracted from their passionate meaning, that they exist only as expressions of a mystery which uses the senses to become manifest. If the *phonai*—the indicative sounds of language—are always originally meaningful, the question of language (*logos*), too, can and must be dealt with on the basis of the fundamental problems just seen.

## 2) The Underivedness of Perceptible Appearances

Spoken words (*phonai*) are the presuppositions of language (*logos*). The remarks which I am about to make are intended to be taken as an attempt to identify the origins of language, that is, they are intend-ed to be propaedeutic to the problem of language. From the Aristote-lian distinction between sound and spoken word—where the latter is understood to be a 'meaningful sound'—there arises the following question: Can we state that sound is transformed into spoken word (*phonē*) when we assign to it an indicative sign (*sema*)? If that were the case, then two factors would be involved in the emergence of a spoken word: a sound (*psophos*) without meaning and our transferral of a meaning or an indication to it. It would be by virtue of these two elements that the new world, the new order—that of language—could emerge. Before disproving the validity of this dualism, let us recall the traditional concept of metaphor.

We must not forget that 'to translate' (to interpret metaphorically, *metapherein*) did not originally have a linguistic meaning, much less a literary one; the term *metapherein* points to the transfer of an object

from one place to another, and that presupposes a 'passage,' a 'cross-
ing,' a 'bridge'.[4] Man must plan for this passage, he must build a
bridge from one place to another, from a here to a there; this action,
in turn, implies a before and an after relating to its realization.
Aristotle in the *Poetics* says that metaphor "consists in giving the
thing a name that belongs to something else."[5] According to Quintilian, metaphor is the result of a mutation (*cum virtute mutatio*).[6]

To transpose meaning from one term to another entails a rejection
of the conceptual definition of beings. Consequently, metaphor is a
far cry from logic; it is therefore placed within an art—such as poetry
or rhetoric—and excluded from philosophy. Hegel wrote that
thought must free itself from the senses and took Humanism to task
for resorting to images, to something natural which, as such, necessarily lacks the nobility of thought.[7] As a result, metaphor is seen as a
'distracting' element which has nothing to do with reality; it is seen
as the expression of the workings of fantasy which at best can be
used—as in medieval thought—as the *integumentum* of rational truth,
to induce those incapable of rigorous thinking into accepting rational
truth: *Fabulas poetae a fando nominaverunt, quia non sunt res factae,
sed tantum loquendo fictae.*[8]

Rabanus Maurus wrote that a poet's task is to translate, with the
help of appropriate images, real events into other forms: *Officium
poetae in eo est, ut ea, quae vere gesta sunt, in alias species obliquis
figurationibus cum decore aliquo conversa transducat.*[9] According to
such thinking, metaphor and poetry are to be seen exclusively as
instruments of the imagination, which has nothing to do with reality.

We can, however, ask ourselves whether this concept of metaphor
is truly valid, whether metaphor should be confined to the realm of
literature and rhetoric and excluded from any form of speculative

---

[4] Herodotus, *Histories*, I, 64; Thucydides, *Histories*, I, 134, 4.
[5] Aristotle, *Poetics*, 1457 b 7; English translation by I. Bywater in *The Complete Works of Aristotle.*
[6] Quintilian, *Institutiones oratoriae* VIII, 6, 1.
[7] G. W. F. Hegel, *Vorlesungen über die Geschichteder Philosophie, in Sämtliche
Werke*, ed. Glockner (Stuttgart: Frommann, 1928), 18:121, 149.
[8] Isidore of Seville, *Etymologiae*, in J. P. Migne, ed., *Patriologica cursus
completus*, Series Latina, (hereafter cited as *P.L.*) (Paris, 1857–1867), 82, I XL, 1.
[9] Rabanus Maurus, *De universo*, in *P.L.* 111, XV, II, 419 c.

thought. Is metaphor simply a game devoid of even the smallest philosophical significance? Ontology—as the rational science of beings, of *onta*—is, for traditional philosophy, the foundation of the science of being, which is to say of metaphysics. Ontology, we claim, enables us to grasp the code of the being of beings. From this we then arrive at the thesis that the problem of different beings is also the problem of being as such which is thereby understood to be the primary original being. Even the theory of knowledge of modern philosophy, which culminates in Kant's "Copernican revolution," begins with beings and then asks through what forms of knowledge beings manifest themselves. But all of this presupposes the duality of object and subject, of *noumenon* and *phenomenon*, of cognitive matter and form, which are the necessary antecedent conditions of any epistemology that finds impossible to understand the *noumenon*. Even in his criticism of Kant, Hegel reaffirms the pre-eminence of the rational nature of reality; according to him, the profound meaning of reality can and must be derived dialectically *a priori*, through the logical process.

Let us now focus our attention on the problem which most interests us. Is the traditional dualistic concept of meaningless sound and spoken word as an indicative semantic sound, as *phoné*, valid? Do we indeed have a sound-producing being preceding all meanings? Only if we answer this question can we ascertain whether the *phoné* consists of a transference, of a transposition of a meaning, of an indicative sign, onto a sound, or whether such a metaphor should be regarded as an originary phenomenon which is not deducible from the sound. In that case, metaphor would have a much more profound meaning and a much more extensive role to play than those traditionally assigned to it.

Once again I turn to Aristotle. He explains sound as a result of a mechanical process: a percussion (the cause) on an entity produces a vibration (the effect) which through a medium, such as water or air, reaches the organ of hearing. We are dealing here with a causal, rational explanation. Aristotle insists on this point, so much so that he goes on to distinguish sound-producing things from others. "Impact on wool makes no sound, while the impact on bronze or any body which is smooth and hollow does."[10] The production of

---

[10] Aristotle, *On the Soul* 419 b 15.

sound is, therefore, a process endured by beings: this is an essentially 'mechanical' explanation. On this matter, we must bear in mind an important Aristotelian passage, often forgotten when dealing with such problems: "When, therefore, we have to do something contrary to nature, the difficulty of it causes us perplexity and art has to be called to our aid. The kind of art which helps us in such perplexities we call mechanical skill."[11] However, by resorting to such a technical-mechanical explanation, do we solve the problem of the *phonê*? The question needs to be answered, since Aristotle himself stated that when we carry something out 'contrary to nature,' we turn to a mechanical explanation.

That the mechanical explanation for sound is in fact untenable is obvious on three counts. First of all, the 'mechanical' explanation leaves out of consideration the fundamental fact that sound depends entirely on an instrument—in our case, the organ of hearing—for its manifestation. It follows that sound can be explained only if we ask what the organ of hearing is an instrument of. Secondly, we must admit that sound always carries a meaning, one which is dependent on whatever the organ is an instrument of. In other words, it is obvious that sound reveals itself to us only within an all-dominating code. Only by knowing the code and by never abstracting from it can we apprehend the meanings of the phenomenon knowable through the senses. Thirdly, the mechanical determination of beings is not identical with the problem of the code, since the same sound can, depending on the code, acquire different meanings: of a call, a threat, an interdiction. The meaning cannot be derived from the sound; it is knowable only within the code of the sense on which the emergence of our world depends.

This last consideration brings forth the importance of the ontological difference, which denies that the problem of beings, rationally defined, is identical with the problem of being as such, and which rejects the possibility of starting from the definition of beings in order to get to their code. This very thesis of the ontological difference commands a new philosophy, different from the traditional one. But, then, where do we begin our new philosophy if we cannot start

---

[11] Aristotle, *Mechanics* 847 a 17–19; English translation by E. S. Forster in *The Complete Works of Aristotle.*

with the abstract rational definition of beings? Where and how does the code manifest itself, that code through which the meaning of sensible reality is revealed? The sound, it has been said, is evidence of the activity, the *ergon*, whose instrument it is. But what activity, what *ergon* are we speaking of? Obviously, it is not a mechanical activity. What follows will further make this clear.

Johannes Müller, the founder of modern physiology, demonstrated that, while different stimuli can give rise to different phenomena in the sense organs, they always cause in each organ the manifestation of the phenomenon which is peculiar to it. Müller called this physiological law the "specific energy of the senses."[12] This, too, is further proof that the meaning of sensible phenomena is not a matter of deduction. Whatever it is that any sound, taste or smell points to cannot be grasped by means of a mechanical consideration, for that would be an abstraction. What appears through the senses, what constitutes the horizon of our world depends on instruments for its manifestations, which is to say that it depends on organs and on a code that impels them from the inside. Within the range of pleasure and pain, which are the sources of passions, we are impelled by the fear that we cannot give adequate expression to whatever is pressing on us and by the hope that we can nonetheless carry out this task. It is, therefore, a question of responding to an appeal from the abyss with us. It may be that this is what Novalis meant when he wrote: "All which is visible is attached to the invisible, the audible to the inaudible, the sensible to the insensible. Perhaps, the thinkable to the unthinkable."[13]

Does the poet not appeal to the passion of the spoken words, of the indicative signs? Is he not, then, within the realm of language, the prophet, the herald of all that already presses in the senses? With the passionate aura of his phonemes, the poet points to a nonrational mysterious world which opens up between two darknesses: the darkness of the groundless *physis*, which is not knowable rationally,

---

[12] J. Müller, *Über die phantastichen Gesichtserscheinungen* (Kablenz: 1826), 45; cf. Th. von Uexküll, "Die Physiologie des J. Müller un die moderne Medizin," *Amtliche Wochenschrift der Medizin* 28 (1958), 614.

[13] Novalis, *Schriften, Zweiter Band, Das philosophische Werk I, Studien zur bildenden Kunst,* ed. R. Samuel, H.-S. Mähl, and G. Schulz (Stuttgart: Kohlhammer, 1981), 650 n. 481.

and the darkness which man enters when he cannot find again, through the code of his senses, his own order and is thus forced to seek a new code.

### 3) Every Sensation is a Meaningful Sensation

Can we really assert that sounds, lights, odors, etc.—perceived through organs sensitive to a call which is rationally underivable and passionately experienced—manifest themselves always laden with meaning? Are we not continuously distracted, shaken by meaningless noises, blinded by dazzling lights? We are, in fact, compelled to admit that every perceptible appearance—from the faintest to the most impetuous—is laden with passionate indications, that is to say with utterances, even when its very manifestation makes it appear devoid of meaning and passionateness.

In 1770, in *Essay on the Origin of Language*, Herder writes: "All violent sensations of his body, and among the violent the most violent, those which cause him pain, and all strong passions of his soul express themselves directly in screams, in sounds, in wild inarticulate tones. A suffering animal, no less than the hero Philoctetus, will whine, will moan when pain befalls it, even though it be abandoned on a desert island, without sight or trace or hope of a helpful fellow creature."[14] Herder maintains this thesis in the first paragraph of his work, but later, in developing his interpretation of the origin and structure of language, he abandons it, and with it, its original significance.

Boredom, fear, pleasure and pain, beckons and repudiations are all expressions, warnings, passionate indicative signs; they are, therefore, sensible phenomena through which we swim, either with sensual enjoyment or with despair. It is in this realm that the original horizon we inhabit opens up, the horizon which enables us to perceive disturbing and previously unheard sounds, to see the visible aspect of the invisible, to feel the paradoxical nature of our world. Meaningless sound is sound that remains unheard and, precisely because of this, is unsettling; unrevealing light is terrifying. Every organic being is preoccupied with what his organs announce and with what appears; he wavers between chaos and cosmos.

---

[14] J. G. Herder, *Essay on the Origin of Language*, tr. A. Gode, in *On the Origin of Language*, ed. A. Gode and J. H. Moran (New York: Ungar, 1966), 87.

For the organic being, that is the being who manifests to himself his world through his organs, there is no sound which is not also a word, no flavor which does not correspond to differentiated taste. Only the terrifying myth of technology, of what is mechanical can assert the aseptic nature of what manifests itself through the senses; that is, the abstract world proposed by rational thought.

Beyond the confines of the senses, there reigns silence, and only abstractions can speak of sounds which are not also words. It is in this sense that Leonardo da Vinci could state that the world is one single living being. Herder writes:

> The surging storm of a passion, the sudden onslaught of joy or pleasure, pain or distress, which cut deep furrows into the soul, an overpowering feeling of revenge, despair, rage, horror, fright, and so forth, they all announce themselves, each differently after its kind. As many modes of sensitivity as are slumbering in our nature, so many tonal modes too.[15]

To reject this sensibility is to die. Passions press on like stormy waters and swarm away like starlings; they impetuously rip and tear the swaying curtains of the wind. Herder goes on to say:

> Now, to be sure, these tones are very simple, and when they are articulated and spelled out on paper as interjections, the most contrary sensations may have almost a single expression. A dull 'ah!' is as much the sound of languid love as of sinking despair; the fiery 'oh!' as much the outburst of sudden joy as of boiling rage, of rising awe as of surging commiseration. [...] The tear which moistens this lusterless and extinguished, this solace-starved eye—how moving is it not in the total picture of a face of sorrow. Take it by itself and it is a cold drop of water. Place it under the microscope, and—I do not care to learn what it may be there. This weary breath—half a sigh—which dies away so movingly on pain-distorted lips, isolate it from its living helpmeets, and it is an empty draft of air. Can it be otherwise with the sounds of feeling?[16]

---

[15] Herder, 89.
[16] Herder, 89–90.

Pain and joy echo and confirm an original and mysterious reality: "The plucked chord performs its natural duty: it sounds! It calls for an echo from one that feels alike, even if none is there, even if it does not hope or expect that such another might answer."[17]

The passionateness of the world perceptible to the senses is the root of our world and constantly returns us to its groundless foundation, which is the abyss. Herder wants to draw us on the vestiges of the abyss, as functions of which our sense instruments are manifest phenomena. We thus find ourselves bent over the mysterious coming to presence of phenomena in order to listen to and identify the meaning of visions, words, images; floating on the waves of the senses, we reach the island of our sensible world, condemned as Philoctetus was, and in the foam of the billows pouring on our shore we seek out the multiplicity of existential occurrence. It is possible to discern a law of nature even, in Herder's words, in this fragmented phenomenal world: "Feel not for yourself alone. But rather: your feeling resound! [...] Do not now touch this weak, this sentient being. However lonesome and alone it may seem to be, however exposed to every hostile storm of the universe, yet is it not alone: It stands allied with all nature!"[18]

## 4) *The Metaphorical* Praxis

We have thus far come to three conclusions. First, our point of departure cannot be the philosophical problem of the rational definition of beings but that of their being. Second, being does not manifest itself in accordance with a rational process; rather, it manifests itself in an originary manner in the passions of a code which is itself passionately experienced, and it realizes itself within the confines of the senses and of the signs of pleasure and pain. Third, the problem of passion therefore precedes that of reason. Having thus inverted the perspective of traditional philosophy, we must now ask ourselves: Where and how do we passionately experience the *objectivity* of being?

In order to answer that question, once again we must begin with a Greek text, the *Cratylus*, which starts with the problem of the objectivity of language, of *logos*. In the *Cratylus*, Plato states the

---

[17] Herder, 89.
[18] Herder, 89.

following thesis: "He [Cratylus] says that they [names] are natural and not conventional—not a portion of the human voice which men agree to use—but that there is a truth or correctness in them. [...] For there is no name given to anything by nature; all is convention and habit of users."[19] Plato takes a stand against the Sophists' relativism, and he begins with experience or *pragma*, with the result of action or *praxis*.

Plato points out that the sophistic thesis, as maintained by Protagoras, that words have a merely conventional and arbitrary meaning, cannot be valid, because we must distinguish between *poneroi* men, that is evil men whose actions cause only pain, and *chreistoi* men, good men.[20] We must, in other words, distinguish between what is harmful and what is useful. It is a question of acknowledging—Plato insists—that everything has its own essence, its own way of being, and that *pragmata*, then, cannot be used at will: "But if ... things are not relative to individuals, and all things do not equally belong to all at the same moment and always, they must be supposed to have their own proper and permanent essence; they are not in relation to us, or influenced by us, fluctuating according to our fancy, but they are independent and maintain to their own essence the relation prescribed by nature."[21] We can only burn what can be burned, cut what can be cut. The passionately experienced code, through whose agency sensible reality manifests itself to us, is neither arbitrary nor subjective: it is ineluctably compelling.

On this matter, Greek philosophy radically distinguishes two forms of action: *poiesis* and *praxis*. Although *poiesis* is an action, it is not an originary action. It is a means for the realization of a product, of an *ergon*, which, however, is not peculiar to it. That is why the action comes to an end once the work is carried out, its purpose accomplished. *Poiesis* is not an activity with an end in itself; it is an instrument and its goal lies not within it, but without it.

*Praxis*, instead, is an originary activity whose product, *ergon*, does not come into being on account of something else but only of what

---

[19] Plato, *Cratylus*, 383 a, 384 d; English translation by B. Jowett in Plato, *The Collected Dialogues*, ed. E. Hamilton and H. Cairns (Princeton, NJ: Princeton Univ. Press, 1961).
[20] Plato, *Cratylus*, 386 b.
[21] Plato, *Cratylus*, 386 l.

is proper to it: "Since of the actions which have a limit none is an end but all are relative to the end ... this is not an action or at least not a complete one (for it is not an end); but that in which the end is present is an action."[22]

What the senses reveal, within the limits of pleasure and pain, does not constitute a product (*ergon*) alien to them. Theirs is neither a mechanical nor poietic activity, but an instance of *praxis*, understood as *parousia*, that is to say the manifestation *par excellence*. What becomes manifest through the *erga* of the senses is their own energy, the result of an action which is peculiar to them.

But what constitutes the metaphorical character of sensible signs? It manifests itself through passion, in whose sphere organic being experiences, within the limits of pleasure and pain, the objectivity of responding or not responding to what the senses are instruments of, namely the abyss. All that appears is either identical or not identical to itself, since it always refers back to what it is an indication of. Each phenomenon is a metaphor of the mystery of organic reality in its diverse situations and in the underivedness of its expressions.

In that sense, everything that is manifested to us by way of our senses attains another meaning, according to the here and now, according to the place and time in which the abyss prevails on us. In the *Philebus*, Plato states that what is pleasant in a situation appears unpleasant in another.[23]

Only if *poiesis* becomes but a moment of *praxis* can we see the metaphorical nature of reality; if it is otherwise, *poiesis*, the action of producing, becomes a game, the proof that we have not reached ultimate reality.

---

[22] Aristotle, *Metaphysics* 1048 b 18–23; English translation by W.D. Ross in *The Complete Works of Aristotle*.

[23] Plato, *Philebus*, 32 d; English translation by R. Hackforth in *The Collected Dialogues*.

# Passion and Illusion

## 1) The Problem of Passion: Freud

The priority accorded by philosophy to rational thought and
hence to rational language implies that passions are to be considered
merely something purely subjective and, consequently, that all poetic,
metaphoric language which attempts to express them is devoid of
value. Passions distract us from the clarity of rational thought and
draw us away from primary being, the object of the metaphysical
quest.

Let us ask the following question: Can we find a contemporary
thinker who always denied that he was a philosopher and who was
never considered one by the philosophers of the idealist tradition,
whom we can re-assess precisely in the context of the problem we are
concerned with?

Sigmund Freud develops his fundamental thesis in his well known
*Formulierung über die zwei Prinzipien des psychischen Geschehens*
(1911).[1] The first principle—which alludes to the originary source of
passion—is expressed as follows: "The governing purpose obeyed by
these primary sources is easy to recognize; it is described as the
pleasure-unpleasure principle, or more shortly the pleasure principle.
These processes strive towards gaining pleasure; psychical activity
draws back from any event which might arouse unpleasure. (Here we
have repression.)"[2]

---

[1] S. Freud, "Formulations on the two Principles of Mental Functioning," in
*The Essentials of Psycho-Analysis*, ed. Anna Freud, tr. J. Strachey (London: The
Hogarth Press, 1986).

[2] Freud, *Essentials of Psycho-Analysis*, 508.

Freud defines this principle as the most ancient, as the primary process, as the residual product of a developmental phase which is originary and underivable. This impulse towards pleasure therefore manifests itself as the groundless origin of passion.

Knowledge of the second principle emerges from an equally fundamental experience. When the impulse towards pleasure remained unsatisfied and disappointed then

> the psychical apparatus had to decide to form a conception of the real circumstances in the external world and to endevour to make a real alteration in them. A new principle of mental functioning was thus introduced; what was presented in the mind was no longer what was agreeable but what was real, even if it happened to be disagreeable. This setting-up of the *reality principle* proved to be a momentous step.[3]

Sorrow and pain appear therefore as the *obvious signs* that the impulse which has been experienced has *elicited no response*. In accordance with this line of thinking, the *world of human beings*—since this is what we are dealing with—is shaped, for Freud, on the one hand, in the context of the satisfactory response to the pleasure principle, and on the other, in the context of the experience of the inability of the individual to respond to the appeal of passion and of its transference to a new form. Consequently, either of two things can occur: sublimation (through art, religion, etc.) or illness—"every neurosis has as its result ... a forcing of the patient out of real life, an alienating him from reality."[4] Hence, this negative, subjective fundamental experience of pain emerges from our inability to placate our longing for pleasure in a concrete situation: "Actually the substitution of the reality principle for the pleasure principle implies no deposing of the pleasure principle, but only a safeguarding of it."[5]

## 2) Is Freud a Philosopher?

We began our discussion, which should lead us to the originary meaning of passions, by rejecting all thinking that prioritizes the

---

[3] Freud, *Essentials of Psycho-Analysis*, 508.
[4] Freud, *Essentials of Psycho-Analysis*, 507.
[5] Freud, *Essentials of Psycho-Analysis*, 514.

question of individual beings, but the Freudian principles of pleasure and reality constitute the outline for a theory of the formation of the world. These principles go beyond the limits of a psychological theory and acquire an essentially philosophical significance; in reality they stand opposed to all aprioristic modes of thinking. In all his writings, however, Freud denies having any philosophical intention. He is a doctor and wishes to explain certain illnesses that cannot be assessed on an organic basis; therefore he always declares that his intent is psychological, not philosophical.

At this point we ask ourselves: Can the Freudian definition of the structure and function of passion be considered a *purely psychological* theory? Another question we can ask is the following: Is it really true that Freud's principles of pleasure and reality have no philosophical basis? He expressly declares:

> It is of no concern to us in this connection to enquire how far, with this hypothesis of the pleasure principle, we have approached or adopted any particular, historically established, philosophical system. We have arrived at these speculative assumptions in an attempt to describe and to account for the facts of daily observation in our field of study [...] On the other hand we would readily express our gratitude to any philosophical or psychological theory which was able to inform us of the meaning of the feelings of pleasure and unpleasure which act so imperatively upon us. But on this point we are, also, offered nothing to our purpose. This is the most obscure and inaccessible region of the mind, and, since we cannot avoid contact with it, the least rigid hypothesis, it seems to me, will be the best.[6]

Can we afford to take lightly the fundamental issue of the passionate experience of existence—by which pleasure and pain give meaning to beings—and assert, as Freud does, that "the least rigid hypothesis will...be the best"? Can we state, in other words, that passions are a *purely psychological* phenomenon? The Freudian explanation of the formation of the world of human beings—through passion, repres-

---

[6] S. Freud, *Beyond the Pleasure Principle*, tr. J. Strackey, ed. G. Zilboorg (New York: Bontem, 1967), 21-22.

sion, sublimation, the reality principle—presupposes an incompatibili-
ty between the groundlessness of passion and the compelling nature
of the analysis of the everchanging forms assumed by passion when
it presents itself objectively. *The world of human beings* can only
emerge in the confrontation between the impulse towards pleasure
and what Freud calls the 'external world" (*Aussenwelt*). The comparison of the passionate subject with the objects in the external world
presupposes, however, the subject-object dualism typical of traditional
philosophy. Therefore, we are again in the realm of philosophy, and
of the most traditional sort at that. It is precisely the *Aussenwelt*
which guarantees the objectivity of the pleasure principle (which we
call the appeal of the abyss) and the objectivity of the world which
derives from it.

## 3) Eros and Thanatos

Freud discussed the pleasure principle in relationship to the problem of death as well (*Eros and Thanatos*). Again we ask: Is it an issue
pertaining exclusively to psychology? Freud writes:

> On the basis of theoretical considerations, supported by biolo-
> gy, we put forth the hypothesis of a death instinct, the task of
> which is to lead organic life back into the inanimate state; on
> the other hand, we supposed that Eros, by bringing about a
> more and more far-reaching combination of the particles into
> which living substance is dispersed, aims at complicating life
> and at the same time, of course, at preserving it.[7]

But how did Plato, for example, develop the eternal question of the
relationship between Eros and Thanatos and the question of sorrow
related to it? It is in the realm of Eros, and precisely when Eros
returns us to a transcendental reality and we thereby manage, according to Plato, to overcome our historicity, that we are able to free
ourselves of the prison of our body. So, for Plato, Eros is intimately
connected with the experience of death since it is precisely through
death, and only through death, that Eros achieves its definitive
confirmation in external, ahistorical space: the realm of the super-
sensory.

---

[7] *The Ego and the Id*, in *The Essentials of Psycho-Analysis*, 462.

Contrary to Plato's thought on this, and contrary to Freud's thesis on the death instinct (interpreted as an impulse different from, or rather contrary to, the pleasure principle) we argue that philosophy can no longer be grounded on the problem of individual beings, but rather on the question of *suffering* and therefore on the passionate appeal of the abyss in whose realm we find ourselves.[8] Since the impulse towards pleasure coincides with the passionate, suffered experience of the appeal of the abyss, and since such an appeal does not emerge as a being pleasurable *in itself*, pleasure and pain, exultation and depression are always connected. Pleasure and pain manifest themselves as two forms joined together at their point of origin so that we may evaluate our response, here and now, to the appeal of the abyss. We can therefore study the question of objectivity only within the context of the 'appeal' and of the process of its becoming, and not merely in the context of a confrontation of pain and pleasure with a distant, separate 'external world'. Existential philosophy warns us against the dualistic conception of pain and pleasure, and of the desire for life and the death instinct. In various situations the pleasure and the pain of the same individual are rooted one in the other: only in this dialectic is reality made manifest. The reality of the intimate relationship between Eros and Thanatos does not constitute only the basis for a psychological theory, nor can it merely be the theme of a literary work. The analysis of this relationship can and must find its confirmation only in the sphere of the essence of our groundless passion.

## 4) *Reality as Illusion: Leopardi*

Does not the insistence on passions, on their status of 'becoming' as it relates to situations and their continuous dawning and setting and hence to the metamorphosis of the meaning of that which appears, of the objects of our passions and of the institutions which attempt to bridle them in different ways according to the various eras and to the various 'chapters' of history, does not this insistence point

---

[8] Cf., for example, my books: *Rhetoric as Philosophy: The Humanist Tradition* (University Park and London: The Pennsylvania State Univ. Press, 1980); *Heidegger and the Question of Renaissance Humanism*, Medieval & Renaissance Texts & Studies, vol. 24 (Binghamton, 1983); *Renaissance Humanism: Studies in Philosophy and Poetics*, Medieval & Renaissance Texts & Studies, vol. 51 (Binghamton, 1988).

to the 'illusory' nature of the 'disclosure' of existence? What is the meaning of our relentlessly repeated agonizing cry for the death of a beloved person, for the end of a passion, for the fall of a historical era? This is the enigma of death. Do we not always try to cling on to what we have achieved and to what we have institutionalized? Ancient myths, however, warn us against the futility of holding on to the meaning of what has been. They warn us against looking backwards: In the Old Testament, a backward glance could turn someone into a pillar of salt, and in Greek mythology it prevented Orpheus from saving Eurydice from Hades.

We can draw, from all this, some pessimistic conclusions: Is our life an illusion? We should deal with this problem at the end of our analysis, but we would like to introduce it here by making some references to Leopardi's *Zibaldone*, a text in which the great themes he later expressed in his poetic compositions appear as philosophical speculations and consequently in ways more pertinent to the theoretical nature of our discourse. The importance of Leopardi's meditations derives from the fact that they originate from his sorrows, unmediated. In delving into the depths of his own pain, he formulates theses quite remote from any aprioristic modes of thinking.

The nonaprioristic character of Leopardi's thought is the very reason for which both Croce and Vossler could never understand it and thus could never acknowledge Leopardi's philosophical aptitude.[9]
Leopardi writes:

> The imagination of the Germans (I am speaking in generalities) being rather unnatural, not altogether their own, and in some ways artificial and inauthetic and therefore false, although very lively, does not possess the spontaneous correspondence and harmoniousness with nature typical of the imaginations that derive from and are generated by nature itself. (The same goes for feeling.) Consequently, such imagination causes them to mistake one thing for another and to dream. And when a

---

[9] Cf. B. Croce, *Poesia e non poesia: Note sulla letteratura europea del secolo decimonono*, fifth ed. (Bari: Laterza, 1950), 97ff.; K. Vossler, *Leopardi*, Italian translation T. Gnoli (Napoli: Ricciardi, 1925). On the question of Leopardi's "philosophy," see also my article "Der italianische Schopehauer," in *Schopehauer im Denken der Gegenwart*, ed. V. Spierling (München—Zürich: Piper, 1987), 125–138.

German wants to theorize and express great thought, when he wants to design a grand system of his own, or make a great innovative contribution to philosophy or to a particular area of it, I dare say that he is merely delirious.[10]

Leopardi juxtaposes reason to what he calls *illusion*: "Reason is the enemy of all greatness: Reason is the enemy of nature: Nature is vast, reason is small. I mean to say that the more a man is dominated by his reason, the fewer are his chances of achieving greatness and the higher is the degree of difficulty he will experience in such endeavor: for few are the men who can achieve greatness (perhaps none in the arts and in poetry) and they will succeed only if they yield to illusions."[11] Illusion is here seen as the painful experience of the appeal of the abyss which is the origin of all human events. This is the very strength of illusion.

Leopardi is opposed to the predominance of reason because reason leads to abstract truth. The defining traits of rationality are *generality*, *sameness*, and *abstraction*, whereas the appeal of beings can only manifest itself in the realm of circumstance:

Since our ideas depend on nothing but the way in which things really are; since they have no reason independent of themselves nor outside of themselves and could have been, therefore, completely different and even the exact opposite; since they derive in all respects from our sense impressions, our assuefactions, etc.; since our judgements, therefore, have in essence no universal, eternal and immutable basis; by virtue of all this, and in recognition of the fact that all is relative and relatively true, we must reject the immensely large number of opinions based on the false—although natural—idea of the absolute. It is an idea, as I stated, which has no possible reason for being, since it is not innate, nor is it *independent of things as they are and of existence*.[12]

Even if truth is general and if reason aims at reducing multiplicity

---

[10] G. Leopardi, *Tutte le opere, Zibaldone di Pensieri*, a cura di F. Flora (Milano: Mondadori, 1937), 1:1178 n. 1853.

[11] Leopardi, 19 n. 14.

[12] Leopardi, 1054. nn. 1617–1618.

to sameness, we do not exist in this abstract realm: we always exist in concrete situations. This is why rational truth leads us to *indifference* and therefore to *tedium*. Nature, which expresses itself in the passion of illusions, imposes its priority on reason. Leopardi maintains that in this context the tragic experience of tedium manifests itself as the experience of one who has lived through the deterioration of passion, as one who cannot respond to its appeal and who cannot reach into its depth: "Tedium is the most sterile of human passions. The daughter of nothingness, it is also its mother: being not only sterile in itself, it makes sterile all it mingles with and all it comes close to."[13] The individual experiences tedium; consequently tedium can be analyzed as a psychological phenomenon, but its essence becomes visible only in the manner in which it relates to the appeal and in the positive or negative responses we succeed in giving it: "Diversity is so hostile to tedium that even diversity in tedium itself is a remedy for it or a relief from it, as we can see, commonly enough, in worldly individuals. On the other hand, continuity is tedium's close ally and continuity in tedium wearies immensely [...]."[14]

According to Leopardi, the difference between man and animal lies in the fact that the behavior of the animal is necessarily determined by nature, whereas man is capable of abstracting himself from the demands of the situations in which he might find himself, thereby distancing himself from nature and succumbing to tedium. Leopardi stresses that everything is relative and that all beings are conditioned by the circumstances in which they exist:

> By committing the natural error of believing that truth is absolute, we think we understand it and we give it the status of an axiom. We attribute to it, to a very large degree, all that we judge to be perfection as well as the need for it not only to be, but also to be in that particular way, namely, the way we deem absolutely perfect. These manifestations of perfection, however, are such only within the order of things we know, that is, within only one of the many possible orders; indeed, merely within some parts of that order, not in others, as I have stated elsewhere in my writings. They are therefore perfections not in

---

[13] Leopardi, 1159 n. 1815.
[14] Leopardi, 78 n. 51.

an absolute but in a relative sense. Nor are they perfections in and of themselves, separate from all else; they are rather relative to the particular nature, purpose, etc, of the beings of which they are an attribute [...]. Surely enough, once we destroy all preexisting Platonic ideas we destroy God.[15]

The sense of priority inherent in each situation or circumstance prompts us to respond to the appeal it issues forth; in other words, we must achieve assuefaction to it: "Not only do all of man's faculties constitute the single faculty of assuefaction, but this same faculty of assuefaction is dependent upon assuefaction itself."[16] In acknowledging the mutable nature of needs, we are compelled to discover new relationships among beings:

> Having stated elsewhere that *ingenium* corresponds to the ease with which one achieves assuefaction, and that this ease implies the readiness to move from one type of assuefaction to another, to develop other forms of assuefaction which contrast with the preceding one, etc., I conclude that men of great intellect (*ingegno*) must ordinarily be extremely versatile (with respect to opinion, taste, style, manner, etc. etc.), not on account of capriciousness born of the superficiality deriving from little intellectual and conceptual strength or from insensitivity, but on account of their readiness towards assuefaction and hence of their ability to develop.[17]

What then is the origin of the world of human beings? It is neither a construct nor a revelation of reason, but rather the product of what Leopardi calls *illusion*, namely, the compelling force of the abyss: without illusion there is no life, no action. Illusion is the origin of history, it always discloses the newness of every era of history: "[...] the things we call great, such as a great exploit for example, usually escape the confines of an order, and their essence is in a certain disorder. Now reason condemns this disorder. Example: the exploits of Alexander: illusion."[18] Great thoughts, great exploits are

---

[15] Leopardi, 903 n. 1342.
[16] Leopardi, 920 n. 1370.
[17] Leopardi, 963–964 nn. 1450–1457.
[18] Leopardi, 19 n. 14.

underivable novelties: "What is the meaning of the fact that so-called barbarians—i.e. nations only half-civilized or whose level of civilization is considered inferior—have always conquered civilized nations, indeed the world? [...] It means that all of man's power is in nature and in illusions."[19] Nature is the representation of illusions: "Illusions are in nature, inherent in the order of the world. Remove them completely or partially and man becomes inhuman."[20] Through the passionateness of illusion, the abyss brings history into being and exorcises continuous change, the continuous becoming of that which appears. In fact, no form of reason exists prior to things and to their mode of being. Against all manner of pessimism, Leopardi tells us that "we search for perfection in the things we see outside of existence, while perfection is here with us, within each category of things known to us, and it would not be perfection in any other possible way."[21] He states further on: "Good is not absolute but relative. It is never absolute in a primary, nor secondary, nor absolute, nor relative sense."[22] Illusion is a necessity of life, but it is shrouded over, in today's world, by the predominance of rational explanations.

## 5) *The Problem of Evil*

On this point we find a contradiction in Leopardi. If the coming to presence of illusions—of the abyss—constitutes the disclosing of history and the opening of a *clearing* in the darkness in which we find ourselves, why then do we think and speak of reality and of illusions as nothingness? "It seems absurd, yet we speak the truth when we say that, all reality being nothingness, there exists in the world nothing real, nothing substantial, other than illusions."[23] Leopardi maintains, therefore, that even illusions must be understood in a negative manner: "[...] he who understands and feels most deeply and painfully the vanity of illusions, honours them, desires them and speaks about them more than anyone else."[24] The wise

---

[19] Leopardi, 580 nn. 866–867.
[20] Leopardi, 32 n. 22.
[21] Leopardi, 1206 n. 1908.
[22] Leopardi, 334 n. 391.
[23] Leopardi, 126 n. 99.
[24] Leopardi, 287–88 n. 318.

man suffers more deeply because he perceives more acutely the vanity of illusions. But Leopardi maintains as well that if man were to follow illusions and the passion inherent in them, he would be less unhappy: it is better to accept a world full of illusory pleasures than to live in a world full of pleasures. Leopardi attempts an explanation of the unhappiness of human existence on many occasions. Man imagines happiness as something infinite, yet all happiness, every pleasure is finite. Man's inclination towards the infinite is, in reality, an inclination towards an abstract unity. The infinite is merely a development, a process of becoming of the finite. Leopardi is well aware of this, yet he writes:

All is nothingness in the world, even my desperation, whose vanity, irrationality and fantasy are acknowledged by all men, even wise men in a tranquil frame of mind and certainly by myself in a more serene state of being. Alas, even this pain I feel is vanity, nothingness, this pain that will eventually vanish and will become nothing and will leave me with a feeling of universal emptiness in a state of terrible indolence that will make me unable even to cry out my pain.[25]

And again "I was terrified to find myself in nothingness, I myself a mere nothing. Thinking and feeling that all is nothingness, solid nothingness, I felt as though I was suffocating."[26]

Can we explain Leopardi's incoherent conclusions only by attributing them to his inability to investigate his problem thoroughly? Must we explain man's suffering, when he is confronted with the transience of all beings, death, the separation from a loved one, only as an inadmissible adherence to beings and as his inability to evaluate correctly the continuous becoming of the being of beings? Are we to explain the tragic, negative evaluation of pain only as the expression of a faulty manner of thinking? What is the purpose of passion? Does it consist in our participating in and our witnessing of the spectacle of events in the world? Does it consist in our looking at the world, in being a part of it and hence in having to accept the pain of annihilation? The lightning flashes in the turbulent storms of history are

---

[25] Leopardi, 103 n. 72.
[26] Leopardi, 112 n. 85.

followed by the fragments of the everchanging experience of the sublime, but they quickly vanish into the menacing, terrifying darkness of evil, because all construction presupposes a new destruction. We are reminded of the Promethean myth and its paradigmatic significance. Every day the eagle devours Prometheus' liver, symbol of the life of the titan, and every night the liver reproduces itself to signify the eternal alternating cycle of construction and destruction and the tragic experience of the eternal relationship between pain and pleasure. As soon as on the stage of existence the most terrible passions have been played through to their ultimate limit, the actors fold limply on themselves like worn-out clothes. The set is struck, the theater is empty. All recedes into silence. The word without passion runs dry. Is this our destiny? To walk forever on an endless path?

In contrast to the way in which Freud later dealt with this issue, Leopardi confronted the problem of passion from a perspective outside any dualism of subject and object. His starting point was his own experience of passion, his concrete personal situation as a man reacting to the appeal of the abyss as it manifests itself through passion. In so doing, he clearly followed a line of thinking different from that of traditional metaphysics. Precisely because of this difference with respect to traditional Platonism (which, as I have pointed out, conditioned Freud's theories), idealist critics have denied Leopardi the status of philosopher. It is clear, however, that Leopardi's theory of illusion—whose necessity and vanity he acknowledged with extreme intellectual clarity—indicates that the human condition is that of being forever thrown into a concrete situation, that of being forever on the brink of the precipice of the here and now of existence. It is a situation which compels him to ask questions whose answers can be neither rational nor universally abstract, for they can only be passionate.

This constitutes the *game* of existence. The game of existence and of its language discloses, in the process of being played, numerous possibilities, forever changing, forever new and unpredictable. As such, they are bound to frustrate man's rational attempt to foresee their meaning. Leopardi's illusion is nothing other than the act of *in-ludersi*, namely the act of involving oneself in the *ludus*, the act of being game to the game; it constitutes the acceptance of the game of existence. The game, as it is being played, allows for the occurrence of situations wherein pleasure and pain, hope and despair show the double, inseparable countenance of a single experience—the experience of passion. As such, it is an experience which deserves more than a psychological explanation; it must be explained philosophically.

Leopardi teaches us that the only philosophy capable of attempting the explanation is a philosophy of existence; namely a philosophy which acknowledges the abyss over which we find ourselves suspended by virtue of our passions. It is a philosophy which does not expect to find rational solutions.

The appeal of the abyss is the appeal of the origin. Novalis—to whose work we shall refer later—yearned incessantly to find again the meaning of this origin and dreamed of a "romanticization of the world." In sharing the same yearning, Leopardi, the theorist of illusions, is his kindred spirit.

# The Theater as a Model
# for the Tragedy of Existence

## 1) The Problem

I would like to begin by asking the following question: Can the structure of the theater, as the place of dramatic and tragic vision (*theoria*) which purports to represent a *story*, an imaginary tale, give us some clues for the formulation of a new philosophy that is not based on the question of individual beings? If it does, what then is the new principle the theater offers us?

If we consider the world of human beings as the object of a *theoria* or a vision, we can readily understand why metaphysics regarded the theater as a metaphor that illustrates its own thought: the reality that man is confronted with is a stage on which God, the first author, gives man the task of representing his own realization in light of his choice to attain or not to attain eternity, thereby losing himself in the becoming of history, which is forever transitory and ephemeral. God presents himself as the creator of our world, as the author of the 'divine comedy' as it is envisaged by Dante. Is this *metaphor* of the world as the creation of a divine *author*, in so far as it is legitimized by the fact that all theatrical works have an author, a valid one? Moreover, is this metaphor validated by traditional philosophy, which seeks to identify the meaning of individual beings in order to grasp the concept of the dominant, creative, first being?

The difference between the metaphysical concepts of the 'theater of the world' and the 'theater of the imagination,' which intends to represent on an imaginary stage a particular setting for the purpose of seeing and revealing the drama and the workings of existence by means of theatrical and metaphorical or rhetorical language, is the following: The theater of the imagination and of literature is considered as the representation of the drama of humanity through arbitrary tales and invented fables that reveal possible stories and unreal, ephemeral worlds on an imaginary stage. Not by chance then, did Aristotle deal with the subject of tragedy and drama in the context of rhetoric rather than in the context of metaphysics.

Since the theater, in its original meaning, is intimately connected with a vision (*theoria*) which is itself linked to the experience of joy and suffering, we can ask ourselves whether reflecting on the theater of the imagination will possibly yield new elements for a philosophy that aims to go beyond the paradigms of traditional metaphysics.

Let us then begin our discussion on the metaphor of the 'theater of the world' by interpreting the first passages of Plato's *Timaeus*. Timaeus asks himself whether the universe has an origin or not.[1] Plato bases his argument on the origin of the world on a series of principles: *First*, philosophy must begin with the problem of individual beings; *second*, the solution to the problem must be arrived at through a rational process; *third*, knowledge based on sense perception or on opinion is fundamentally different from rational knowledge—the first type of knowledge is concerned with the becoming of reality, the second concerns eternal, subsistent reality; the first type of knowledge belongs to the realm of the flow of time, the second belongs to the realm of the atemporal, of "that which always is and has no becoming."[2] To know eternity we need to "think rationally," whereas to know the becoming of the individual being "which never really is" we need to have 'opinions' which derive from nonrational sensations.[3]

From this thesis Plato deduces the necessity to acknowledge the existence of a creator, of a demiurge with a double function: a *poietic* function, which issues forth individual beings from nonexistence into existence, and an *ordering* function by which the process of coming into being of individual beings occurs in accordance with an eternal

---

[1] Plato, *Timaeus*, 27 c; English translation by B. Jowett, in Plato, *The Collected Dialogues*, ed. E. Hamilton and H. Cairns (Princeton, NJ: Princeton Univ. Press, 1961).

[2] Plato, *Timaeus*, 27 d.

[3] Plato, *Timaeus*, 28 a.

model, an eternal paradigm[4] which discloses itself in an exemplary manner through the division of day and night, thereby marking the rhythm of the becoming of time.[5]

Hence Plato legitimizes the possibility of starting from the concept of a theater of individual beings in order to examine carefully their process of manifestation; after all, individual beings are participants in being. We are dealing here with the formulation of a *theorein*, a theater that allows us to see and to discover reality in its entirety. When we speak of the 'theater of the world' we are not using a metaphor arbitrarily; in fact, traditional philosophy has made ample use of it. We must now ponder, however, on the legitimacy of the Platonic explanation concerning the duality of individual beings and the duality of time—transitory and eternal—based on the premise of a demiurge, creator and ordering force of our theater.

First of all, let us emphasize the fact that Plato's theses, in this particular text, are grounded on his conviction of the priority and legitimacy of rational, causal thinking. There are no doubts about this. Plato writes: "Let me tell you then why the creator made this world of generation."[6]

Causal thinking, however, will not lead us to the formulation of any model that will enable us to interpret phenomena: The succession of phenomena will lead us always and only to the reason for the succession of all individual beings. It will never allow us to unveil their meaning. The causal explanation of a sound, a color, a flavor does not provide an answer to the questions concerning its meaning, to whether it signifies a threat, a warning or a suggestion; consequently, the principles of the demiurge and of the distinction between a historical and an ahistorical world are invalidated by the insufficiency of rational thought. It is for this reason that in the *Timaeus* the Platonic attempt to raise the curtain for the purpose of disclosing the great theater of the world fails miserably.

At this point we can ask ourselves the following questions: What is the process that will lead us to the objective meaning of individual beings if we cannot get to it by means of a causal explanation of their

---

[4] Plato, *Timaeus*, 29 a–c.
[5] Plato, *Timaeus*, 37 e.
[6] Plato, *Timaeus*, 29 d–e.

succession? How can we understand the meaning of individual beings through which we realize our everchanging historical world? Could a new interpretation of drama and tragedy help us in ways that the traditional interpretation of tragedy never could, since it hindered our understanding?

## 2) The Symbolic Nature of Pragmatic Activity

Our negation of the Platonic solution regarding the theater of the world is in no way the result of a polemical attitude towards religious tradition which characterizes all of European history. Its source is a far deeper concern.

Existence situates us in a context in which we passionately experience the appeal of the abyss, an appeal which we cannot explain away rationally. Our five senses are the vehicles, the instruments through which passionate experience manifests itself in a primal, originary way. Through the senses we act out our existence. This manifestation is never abstract, it always occurs in concrete situations, in a time and place, in pain and pleasure, in the realm of significant, indicative phenomena. The mechanical underivedness of the meaning of sound, of its originary indicative character—common to all the senses—shows us how we are continuously urged to respond to the signals of the abyss, to react to a compelling semantic system of appeals that must be experienced passionately. This constitutes the game we must play, our theater of existence.

Let us for the moment leave the problem of the theater, and attempt, on the basis of questions that will gradually arise as we go along, to understand our very need to solve such problem. The fundamental experience through which we realize our existence consists of our passionate sensory response to the appeal of the abyss, whose signals are those of pleasure and pain. But in what context do we experience *the objectivity* of the appeal of the abyss? In other words, where and how, in our played out theatrical experience, do we passionately experience, in an originary manner, the objectivity of the being of individual beings? Our question—and we turn back to our reflections at the end of the previous chapter—can now have a precise answer. All that appears in our originary theater, whose curtain is raised by sounds, lights, odors and tastes, coincides with the appearance of the ineluctability of *praxis* (practice), which manifests itself in life through indicative sounds whose originary echo reaches the spoken elements of language.

We must first point out that the examples cited by Plato in his *Cratylus*, through which he defined the experience of objectivity in the context of *praxis*, are not causal in nature, as we might first infer. We authentically build our originary world through a process of burning and cutting, of destroying and cutting again. Therefore, objectivity reveals itself in the immediacy of our existential actions.

Secondly, it is clear that not all cutting and burning, in which objectivity manifests itself, is useful. It is so only in accordance with the situation in which we find ourselves. Hence, an abstract, rational definition of the two actions is insufficient.

Thirdly, only by starting with the experience of the objectivity of being can we come to understand the meaning of individual beings. This implies the acknowledgement of the priority of the ontological difference between being and beings.

In order to solve the problem of the theater of the world we must do more than relate it to the concept of *aletheia*, understood as the rational truth of individual beings. We need to study it in the context of the manifestation and of the revelation of the meaning of beings as it relates to *praxis*, to actions, to the human drama. Consequently, the theater of the world does not appear before us when we raise the curtain on a stage where individual beings stand rationally fixed, abstracted from situations and on whom we look as mere spectators. We ourselves are drawn onto the stage of the theater of the world by the power of the *praxis* of life and not by the *poiesis* of a demiurge. Objectivity manifests itself in the unfolding of our coming into being, through our actions in history.

## 3) Language as Originary Praxis: *The Problem of* Mimesis

Throughout our previous analysis we have made continuous reference to the appeal of the abyss, in response to which our world is generated. But where exactly does such coming into being present itself with the urgency of a theater, understood as the realm of a vision of an ordered system?

The first definition of the essence of tragedy given by Aristotle is the following: "Tragedy is the imitation of an action."[7] He specifies

---

[7] Aristotle, *Poetics*, 1449 b 24; English translation by I. Bywater, in *The*

further: "In a dramatic, and not in a narrative form."[8] What is the meaning of *mimesis*? Its etymological derivations are significant.

According to Boisacq's dictionary, the etymology of *mimesis* is obscure.[9] We find that in Aeschylus[10] and in Euripides[11] the word is used in its verbal form with the meaning of 'imitation'. In Koller we find that the term means 'imitation,' but that it also denotes a wider range of meaning than mere *imitatio*.[12] We discover that the term was used in the context of the dance and that it primarily means 'to represent through dancing'. Therefore, *mimeisthai* must remain linked to the fundamental meaning of 'representing'. Only from this perspective is the distinction between 'to imitate' and 'to represent' linguistically unquestionable.[13]

However, this etymological derivation has been generally forgotten in favor of the term's first meaning and all the difficulties that issue from it. Robortellus, one of the principal commentators of Aristotle's *Poetics*, translated *mimesis* as 'imitation': "*Tragoedia est imitatio actionis illustris.*"[14] Castelvetro translates it as "resemblance".[15] Victorius gives it the same meaning: "*Est autem actionis quidem imitatio fabula.*"[16]

Koller's thesis, in which 'representation by means of dancing' constitutes the principal meaning of *mimesis*, is an important one, for it indicates the essential point of our argument.

On this issue we will refer to Georgiades's fundamental study entitled *Musik und Rhythmus bei den Griechen*.[17] This author points

---

*Complete Works of Aristotle*, the revised Oxford translation, ed. J. Barnes, vol. 2 (Princeton, NJ: Princeton Univ. Press, 1984).

[8] Aristotle, *Poetics*, 1449 b 27.

[9] E. Boisacq, *Dictionnaire étymologique de la langue grecque*, fourth ed. (Heidelberg: 1950); M. W. Prellwitz, *Etymologisches Wörterbuch der griechischen Sprache*, second ed. (Gottingam: 1905).

[10] Aeschylus, *Choephoroe*, n. 564.

[11] Euripides, *Ion*, n. 1429; *Helen*, 875 n. 74.

[12] H. Koller, *Die Mimesis in der Antike. Nachahmung, Darstellung, Ausdruck* (Bern: Froncke, 1954), especially 11.

[13] Koller, 119.

[14] F. Robortellus, *In librum Aristotelis de arte poetica explicationes* (Basel: 1555), 45.

[15] L. Castelvetro, *Poetica d'Aristotele* (Napoli: 1570).

[16] F. Victorius, *Commentarii in primum librum Aristotelis de Arte Poetarum* (Florentiae: 1560), 60.

[17] Th. Georgiades, *Musik und Rhythmus bei den Griechen. Zum Ursprung der*

out that the ancient Greek language contains an essential, determining element: The length and shortness of the vowels in each word are totally independent of the feelings with which the words are pronounced and of the situation in which they are uttered.

Since the succession of long and short vowels determines the rhythm of the language, and language partakes of music and poetry, then language—ancient Greek in this case—is included, from the very beginning and as an entity in itself, in an ordered system and therefore in a rhythm of its own. Moreover, as such, it constitutes the expression and the representation of the passionate experience of that system; consequently, if the Greek poet speaks of a rhythm, he must necessarily express that rhythm not merely *subjectively* through the passionateness of his own individual situation, but he must also acknowledge the objectivity of rhythm, of vowels, of words. In his choice of words he must subject his own subjectivity to the objectivity of language. Only then will his rhythmic language correspond to the rhythm of all language and hence to the objectivity itself that is manifest within it: This is *mimesis* as *representation*, as the manifestation of the originary compelling force of objectivity.

Furthermore, language—essentially a musical and poetic reality—moves in harmony with the movements of the body, it determines the raising (*arsis*) and the lowering (*thesis*) of the foot. From this we derive the so called 'foot' of the verse, namely, a certain coming together of long and short syllables. For example, the *dactyl*—a type of verse characterized by a foot in descending rhythm—is formed by one long syllable and two short syllables (—⌣ ⌣).

This is essentially what language is about: rhythm corresponding to movement. The unit comprising language and dance constitutes the concept of *mousiké*.

We can conclude, then, that the language of the theater is as well the originary expression of a *theorein* experienced in and expressed by language as originary *praxis*. This becomes even more evident when the actor, by donning a mask which conceals his individuality, stresses in speaking his *nonsubjectivity*. Georgiades states that the language spoken by the tragic actor is a masked language in the same way as the actor himself on stage is a man concealed behind a mask.

---

*abendländischen Musik* (Hamburg: Rowohlt, 1958).

The importance of Georgiades's analysis of this matter must indeed be stressed: "The corporality and the objectivity of the Greek language, its independence of subjective will, its mysterious essence and its hidden origins actualized in body movement, all these render it supremely effective. The word, not merely spoken or sung, becomes real through the body and acquires thus a magical presence. Nothing comparable to this is possible with any of the modern languages of the Western world."[18]

We must take the term theater here to signify the disclosing, the seeing and the being seen of the objectivity of *mimesis* meant as process of manifestation. In the theater it is not the single mortal human being, it is not the individual being who speaks, but the power of language as the expression of objectivity, as the expression of being. In the realm of this theater the ontological difference between being and individual beings emerges unexpectedly. Aristotle, however, does not define tragedy merely as the *mimesis* of an action and as the means through which human action and the human drama are made to appear in and for *praxis*. He also states categorically that *myth* "is the first essential, the life and soul ... of tragedy."[19] How, then, is myth the dominant principle of tragedy?

## 4) Rhythm and Myth

In order to understand the full meaning of the term 'myth' and to define the originary context in which it must be discussed, we will examine one of Plato's texts.

In his *Laws*, Plato points out that the process of becoming is typical of individual beings and that rhythm is "order in movement."[20] In other words, every phenomenon mediated by the senses indicates that the process of becoming (meaning both movement in space and metamorphosis, change) must be regulated. *Ruthmós* deriving from *reo*, meaning 'to flow,' 'to move along,' concerns temporal order. Consequently, *ruthmós*, a periodic return at regular intervals,

---

[18] Georgiades, 40.

[19] Aristotle, *Poetics*, 1450 a 38.

[20] Plato, *Laws*, 653 d; English translation by A. E. Taylor, in Plato, *The Collected Dialogues*, ed. E. Hamilton and H. Cairns (Princeton, NJ: Princeton Univ. Press, 1961).

acquires a cosmic meaning related to the succession of day and night and to the cycle of the seasons.

In light of Georgiades's thesis on language, this implies that rhythm is the source of measure (length and shortness) of the verse and the ordering principle of its syllables and of the sounds of its words.[21] In Plato, for example, *ruthmiké* was the term used for all disciplines preliminary to prosody.[22] Furthermore, rhythm encompasses a wide range of human phenomena: the regularity of body movements constitutes the dance; the ordered system of sounds (high and low tones) constitutes melody; the regular succession of sounds and voices constitutes the rhythm of songs. Hence rhythm provides the structure of music and poetry. The Muses open wide the human horizon; consequently, *mimesis* in dance, poetry and music is the representation of order, of the process of becoming, of the coming to presence of that which constitutes the ornament of the cosmos.

In the *Laws*, Plato also states that 'the gods, in their compassion for the hardships incident to our human lot, have appointed the cycle of their festivals to provide relief from this fatigue, besides giving us the Muses, their leader Apollo, and Dionysius to share these festivals with us and keep them right, with all the spiritual sustenance these deities bring to the feast.''[23]

Thus, song and dance, together with *mimesis* (representation) give to sounds and movements the regularity, the order, the sensory concreteness through which humanity can become a part of the sacred choir and hence participate in the order of eternity. Song, dance and rhythm (order) are the origins of ritual.

The uncertain etymology of the word 'ritual'[24] is related to the Greek term *arithmós*, meaning number and to the Sanskrit word *rtám*, meaning the order implicit in religion, an order manifested both by the cosmos and by the social community, as well as by individual experience. *Ritus* doesn't mean, therefore, only an isolated act which establishes a relationship with the sacred. It constitutes, rather, the norm, the provision necessary for such an act to occur. By

---

[21] Aristotle, *Poetics*, 1448 b 21; *Rhetoric*, 1408 b 29.

[22] Plato, *Republic*, 400 b.

[23] Plato, *Laws*, 653 d.

[24] Cf., for example, *Enciclopedia filosofica* (Firenze: Sansoni, 1982), 7:156.

virtue of the provision, the act acquires dignity and effectiveness. Let us not forget that Servius defines ritual as follows: *"aut institutus religiosus aut cerimoniis conservatus."*[25] Isidore of Seville writes: *"Ritus [...] ad justitiam pertinet, quasi rectum, ex quo pium, aequum, sanctumque."*[26] Through ritual, the total human being, existing in a social and historical situation, becomes part of an originary, sacred reality on the occasion of a birth, a marriage, or a death.[27]

Pertinent to this is Georgiades's reference to Pindar's twelfth ode (*Pitica*): Athena, compassionate of human suffering and lamentation, gives man a musical instrument, the *aulos*.[28]

With an instrument, the means by which he can transfer the subjectivity of his sorrow onto a regulated form of *mousiké* (a unit combining dance, language and music), man in ritual is able to unveil the world and the order of the cosmos.

What connection is there between ritual and Aristotle's thesis that myth is the *arché*, the generating principle of tragedy meant as the revelation of human *praxis*? Is there in the meaning of myth enough of an ambiguity that allows us to interpret it as objective and therefore sacred, or as subjective and therefore historical? On the one hand, myth means word, sacred tale; on the other, it means word, individual, imaginary tale.

The original meaning of myth implies speaking and thinking in a manner not unrelated to doing. In Homer, for example, it means simultaneously *event* and reality.[29] Plato, however, changes profoundly Homer's meaning of myth. Myth acquires the meaning of speaking 'not altogether truthfully," or even of telling things that are not true; consequently, myth (tale) no longer retains the dignity of true speech and hence contrasts with *logos*.

The ambiguity inherent in the term *mythos* was emphasized by the philologist Walter F. Otto. In reference to Homer, Otto reminds us

---

[25] Servius, *In Vergilii Aeneidos librum duodecimum Commentarius*, 12:836, ed. G. Thilo (Hildesheim: Olms, 1961), 2:644–45.

[26] Isidore of Seville, *Differentiae*, in *P.L.* 83, I, 18, 122.

[27] Cf. for example J. Cazeneuve, *Les rites et la condition humaine d'après des documents ethnographique* (Paris: PUF, 1958).

[28] Th. *Georgiades*, 9ff.

[29] Homer, *Iliad*, 18, 5. 252.

that myth *vis-à-vis* logos is not merely the most ancient expression, but it also corresponds to a most ancient concept. It is the word as immediate witness to that which was, is and will be. In other words, it is the revelation of being in all its venerable and ancient significance, whereby the word is all one with that which manifests itself at the origin through verbal expression.[30] *Logos* designates the word from the subjective perspective of the thinker and the speaker, and therefore it is concerned with what is thought and what is designated. Instead, in a completely different sense, in an objective sense, myth means the word which designates "the real, the actual."[31] Let us keep in mind that according to Aristotle's definition, myth is the principal element of tragedy, the one which governs the other five: "characters, diction, thought, spectacle and melody."[32]

Throughout our discussion we have always referred back to the appeal of the abyss in response to which our world comes into being. Such an indicative, urgent appeal presents itself in the theater through myth. It is precisely through myth that the other five elements acquire different meanings in each theatrical performance.

Myth is therefore an *arché*, the principle that governs the meaning of tragedy. It is not a cause, an *aitia*. In fact, only within the context of myth can we ask the question about the causes of the succession of single events, and it is the answer to this question that will lead us to cognitions, validated exclusively by myth itself as it varies in each tragedy. A personal preoccupation, an individual passion of the actor, existing outside of the myth in which he situates himself as an actor performing his action, would destroy the theatrical work altogether. If the individual actor worries about his own death or the death of another actor—preoccupations which are unrelated to the myth he is representing on stage—he destroys the atmosphere created as the tale unfolds and steps out of character. He must be continuously dominated by the plot, he must subject himself to the exigencies of the chain of causes and effects (the *aitiai*) as they reveal themselves in the

---

[30] W. F. Otto, *Gesetz, Urbild und Mythos* (Stuttgart: J. B. Metzler, 1951), now in *Die Gestalt und das Sein. Gesommelte Abhandlungen über den Mythos und Seine Bedentung für die Menscheit* (Darmstadt: Wissenschaftliche Buchgesellschaft, 1955), 6ff.

[31] Otto, 68.

[32] Aristotle, *Poetics* 1450 a 8.

context of the myth (*arché*). In tragedy, myth discloses the occurrence of a manifestation, of a *parousia* in which the process of becoming of causes and effects is sustained by the tension characteristic of the narrative of myth, considered as an originary compelling need (*arché*). The need felt by the actor to act out the plot, the plot being the *arché*, derives from his absolute submission to myth. This is why the theme, the language, the characters, the musicality of the performance, and even its spectacle acquire in every myth a new meaning.

We must therefore acknowledge the presence of two forms of becoming in the theatrical manifestation of myth. First, the temporal development of the event within the context of myth is a time which raises the constituents of the theater from a subjective to an objective level within the structure of the plot. Second, and radically distinct from this time which we will call dramatic, is another temporal manifestation: the birth, development and death of the creative imagination of the author who, through this process, is able to plan and realize a story.

At this point, mindful of the difference between *praxis* and *poiesis*, of the concept of *mimesis* as representation rather than imitation, and of the double meaning of myth (fable and compelling objectivity), we must ask the following question: What are the originary modes of revelation of our world? According to the surprising formulations we found in the *Cratylus*, our world reveals itself through the compelling power of objectivity present in our actions and in individual beings, taken not as something available and usable, but as *pragma*.

The theater of existence can be seen and heard, and in this it is different from the theater of the imagination, whose story is invented by the individual and is thus the creation of a demiurge existing outside of the performance. We participate in the theater of existence as actors and spectators by unfolding our drama through a pragmatic process which we experience in the fusion of sorrow and joy and which shows us the everchanging aspects of objectivity. We are thus obliged to acknowledge that myth, both sacred and literary, corresponds to the being that urges all individual beings. They appear on the stage of our world and on the stage of our imagination as entertainment, as the literary distortion of the tragic dimension of our existence. In his theory of tragedy, Aristotle expresses clearly the theme of ontological difference by stating that knowledge of myth (the essence of tragedy) cannot be deduced from its constitutive elements (individual beings).

He strengthens his thesis by stating that only beginners and bad authors think they are able to write a tragedy on the basis of a discussion of ideas, for example, rather than on the basis of myth. Only on the basis of myth can ideas attain their full dramatic significance, only in this way can they acquire the full meaning of action.

# The Experience of the Word

## 1) Consciousness of the Ontological Difference

In the preceding remarks I have tried to legitimate two theses: 1) the impossibility of starting with the problem of individual beings to get to the definition of being as such; 2) the acknowledgement of the fundamentally pathic nature of the meaning of reality. The 'passion' in this does not derive from our deeply felt perceptions of individual things, but from our suffered experience of an impelling call of the abyss, by virtue of which reality comes to originary presence, exists, and perishes, within the limits of pleasure and pain as apprehended through the senses. This is reality understood as *physis*, as the disclosure of worlds. Both theses are based on an awareness of the ontological difference.

In contrast to Heidegger's thesis, in this study I have stressed that in ancient thought consciousness of the ontological difference appears next to the ontological tradition. My comments on Aristotle's definition of tragedy are a continuous effort to shed light on this particular point. However, medieval thought, in those instances where it is critical of tradition, displays an awareness of the ontological difference as well.

On this point, Meister Eckhart's formulations prove exemplary. Keeping to beings, holding on to them, so to speak, means forgetting being as such and being satisfied with 'Nothingness' instead; it means not recognizing the symbolic and metaphorical nature of individual beings. "In all gifts and in all works . . . we must never stop at these things. In no way do we have a fixed point in this life."[1] He who starts with the problem of individual beings and causal thought will be driven on from one being to the next, in the concatenation of cause and effect, and will be forever limited to asking 'why,' without ever reaching either the original problem of being or its solution: "Those who act in order to know why are *servants and mercenaries.*"[2] A philosophy of the originary cannot ever find its point of departure in any form of ontology: "Everything that the soul produces is produced through its faculties; what it knows, it knows it through its reason ... and so it operates through faculties and not through being."[3] The soul, then, operates "through its faculties," "through its reason" and not through being. But what do these phrases mean? Being as being cannot ever be apprehended through the isolated rational determination of individual beings, since being as such is not a being but an 'other,' and individual beings, in their meaningfulness, are 'transpositions' of this 'other'. Being "is neither this nor that, and yet it is something higher than this or that ... Therefore I now call it in a more noble manner than I have done before, and yet nobility means nothing to it."[4] Being and wisdom in this regard have both the nature of the abyss: "The entire wisdom of the angels and of all living beings is only madness in comparison with the unfathomable wisdom of the Father."[5]

In another study[6] I have tried to show how negative theology displays the awareness that it is illegitimate to start with the issue of individual beings to come to the definition of being.

The tradition of medieval thought, moreover, not only includes the consciousness of the ontological difference, but also contains the thesis of the originary character of the 'word,' with its dominance and urgency, which are independent of any prior rational determina-

---

[1] Meister Eckhart, *Deutsche Predigten und Traktate*, ed. J. Quint, C. Hanser (München: 1955), Treatise 21, 89.

[2] M. Eckhart, *Die deutschen Werke*, ed. J. Quint (Stuttgart: Kohlhammer, 1971), vol. 2, Sermon 39, 253.

[3] M. Eckhart, *Deutsche Predigten und Traktate*, Sermon 57, 416.

[4] M. Eckhart, *Die deutschen Werke*, vol. 1, Sermon 2, 39.

[5] M. Eckhart, *Die deutschen Werke*, vol. 2, Sermon 52, 486.

[6] *La preminenza della parola metaforica. Heidegger, Meister Eckhart, Novalis* (Modena: Mucchi, 1987).

tion of beings. The word is an expression of the sense of urgency which comes to us from the abyss.

I am thinking of Nicholas of Cusa here, of his *Dialogus de Deo abscondito*. It is, as is well known, a dialogue between a Christian and a 'Gentile,' who here personifies the advocate of rational thought. It is surprising to find that, in this dialogue, Cusanus categorically states that the rational process, which presupposes the duality of subject and object, cannot lead to an original knowledge: "... In fact, if I question you on the substance of what you think you know, you will reply that you can't express the truth as such about man and stones. But if you know that man is not a stone, you know it not by virtue of a science which presumably taught you about man, stones, and the difference between them, but by accident, by virtue of their diversity in shape and actions. Having discerned these, you establish names for them. Names, in fact, are determined by an act of discerning reason."[7] Nicholas of Cusa insisted on this point of his critique: the duality of subject and object *is not originary*: "But how can truth be apprehended if not in itself? We would not apprehend it at all if there were, on the one hand, he who apprehends it and, on the other hand, that which is apprehended."[8]

What is our point of departure, then, in our own philosophy? In contrast to the rationalist, the Christian starts with a 'passion': the dialogue opens with the Christian crying, and the rationalist's surprise originates precisely from the fact that he notices his interlocutor's despair. His are tears of despair which—as the text emphasizes—*come from the heart*. It is this despair which exorcises the first lines of the dialogue: "Gentile: I see you prostrate with great devotion, shedding true tears of love which come from your heart."[9] The rationalist is astonished: "Gentile: What do you worship? Christian: God. Gentile: Who is this God you worship? Christian: I don't know. Gentile: Why do you worship with such seriousness what you don't know ?"[10] The rationalist's astonishment springs from the fact that the point of departure of his philosophy is always an *object*, the

---

[7] Nicholas of Cusa, *Dialogus De Deo abscondito*, in *Scritti filosofici*, ed. G. Santinella (Zanichelli: Bologna, 1980), vol. 2, 57.

[8] Ibid.

[9] Nicolas of Cusa, 55.

[10] Ibid.

attempt to explain this object rationally. However, it is this very attempt which prevents him from apprehending the grief felt by the Christian, who does *not start with an object*, but with a passion. What passion could this be?

The Christian takes the opposite stand and articulates it, polemically enough, through an astonishment of his own: he finds it surprising that one could start with a science (*scire*), based on the rational definition of an object. He calls it a folly:

> Gentile: I find it strange that a man should feel affection for what he doesn't know. Christian: It is stranger that a man should feel affection for what he believes he knows. Gentile: Why? Christian: Because he knows what he believes he knows less well than what he is certain he doesn't know. Gentile: Please, tell me why. Christian: Since nothing can be known, I consider a fool anybody who thinks he knows something.[11]

A passion, then, marks the beginning of Cusanus's dialogue, a passion which has nothing to do with any form of onto-logy or logic, and everything to do with the binding force it wields, with the impelling need to be painfully and passionately aware of one's own ignorance (a topic dear to Aristotle himself).

But how does Cusanus give this compelling force actuality of shape and form in his dialogue? The answer is unequivocal, removed from any logical inference: this binding force, 'passionately experienced,' manifests itself—unexpectedly for us—in the word's ineluctable self-assertion, in the attestation of its original, rationally underivable power. The manifestation of the meaningful signs of our senses is not the result of our abstract knowledge, but occurs in the very act in which the abyss imposes its appeal on man, something which, according to Cusanus, takes place precisely because man is *zoon logon echon*. In this definition, *logos* is not reason, but it is the original compelling force of the *word*.

When his interlocutor asks him what God is, the Christian replies: "I know that all which I know is not God, all which I think is not similar to him, that he is beyond it all."[12] This statement prompts

---

[11] Ibid.
[12] Nicholas of Cusa, 59.

the gentile to conclude: "Hence God is nothingness." To which the Christian replies: "God is not nothingness, since this very nothingness has a name: nothingness."[13]

Cusanus's thesis, then, can only make sense in light of consciousness of the ontological difference which manifests itself in the being of beings, and which impels us and imposes itself on us in the *need* to give names to things. This imposition gives rise to *oboedientia*: that which exists complies, through the word, with being as being: "And this is his omnipotence, by virtue of which he is superior to all which is and to all which is not, so that all which is, as well as all which is not, might obey him."[14] Being, then, originally becomes manifest through *contradiction*, since the Christian states that it manifests itself in all individual beings while, at the same time, it is not any of them: "But God is not something in particular rather than all things."[15] Being does not adhere to the principle of identity: it is not a thing, but, at the same time, it is not nothing. It becomes manifest as a mystery in the need to name things.

The *oboedientia* of individual beings is nothing but the consequence of the preeminence of being, one which is passionately and existentially experienced in the ontological difference, which is itself seen as the ungrounded mysterious key to the manifestation of reality. The ontological difference, then, must not be considered only a speculative theory underlining the underivedness of being from individual beings; it is, rather, the *code* which asserts itself in order to reveal being as being, in its groundless and mysterious structure, through and in language.

At this point, we can draw one further fundamental conclusion: If, for the reasons advanced by Cusanus, rational definitions do *not lead* to the knowledge of reality, then language arises out of our individual experiences of being in concrete situations. Consequently, the history of this dialogue on being (which for Cusanus is God, for us ungrounded reality) is our history, the history of our language and of the manifestations of the various *kosmoi* which follow one another.

This dialogue both affirms something and denies it at the same

---

[13] Ibid.
[14] Nicholas of Cusa, 61.
[15] Nicholas of Cusa, 59.

time, in the manner in which one responds, in every situation, to the
call of the abyss, in the manner in which every statement is, simultaneously, identical and nonidentical with itself, since it always refers
back to being as such, which is never the same as the name of any
individual being. The 'code,' then, through which we arrive at the
meaning of individual beings, is not arbitrary, since every situation
must be read in terms of being's imposition of itself on us.

Given all we have said, it is now easier to understand why Cusanus would call his philosophy a *docta ignorantia.* Ignorance of
individual beings and denial of the preeminence of rational science
lead us to a *docta ignorantia*, that is, a *doctrina* which has nothing to
do with any form of onto-theo-logical metaphysics.

## 2) The Problem of the Term 'Sublime' in Pseudo-Longinus

How can we further develop the underivedness of language, the
act of speaking as an original passion, the concept of language as a
means of rising above the multiplicity of beings, and confer truth on
the reality of the word, sublimating it?

The term 'sublime' is a dangerous one. In order to illustrate just
how dangerous it is, I shall quote the first lines of Schiller's essay on
the sublime written in 1793:

> We call sublime an object whose representation causes our
> sensory nature to become aware of its limits, while our rational
> nature is aware of its superiority and its freedom from limits;
> an object which gets the best of us physically, while morally,
> by means of ideas, we rise above it.[16]

Schiller's essay aims at playing down the importance of our
sensory nature to which he opposes the rational world of ideas,
supposedly the source of our freedom. Schiller insists on this dualism
and soon after states: "As sensory beings we are not independent, as
rational beings we are free." Schiller, in asserting this dualism of
sensibility and rationality, and especially in maintaining the pre-
eminence of the latter, expresses the central concept of idealism.
Language must rise above the perceptible; it should take on the task

---

[16] Friedrich Schiller, *Vom Erhabenen*, in *Werke*, 12, 1, *Kleinere philosophische
Schriften*, ed. R. Boxberger (Berlin-Stuttgart: Spemann, 1882).

of overcoming the presumed duality of mind and nature and of unifying it. Sensibility is to be rendered sublime through artistic, literary, and poetic language; it is to be spiritualized through a new expression which, albeit a nonconceptual one, belongs nevertheless to philosophical discourse. That is the concept from which Schiller derived his theory of man's aesthetic education, and his assessment of the different artistic genres. A great many issues of German idealism are contained in the definition of that word which Schiller termed 'sublime'.

We must, however, ask ourselves: Can we proceed differently, go beyond Schiller's conclusions, and illustrate the originary character, the groundlessness, and the underivedness of language experienced as the revealing power of our existential reality?

In order to discuss this problem, I shall now refer to the work entitled *On the Sublime* (*Perí hypsous*) attributed to Longinus. This work is difficult to classify. The fact that its starting point is the *word*, rather than the issue of individual beings, makes it impossible to place it within the sphere of traditional philosophy, which regards the problem of language as nonsensical. On this basis, the text should be denied its philosophical character, and this, in fact, is exactly what has happened.

The treatise *On the Sublime* cannot be counted among the texts dealing with metaphysical speculation nor, strictly speaking, among those pertaining to traditional rhetoric. A 'persuasive' work, in fact, always presupposes the affirmation of a logical truth: the rhetorician's task is to activate, in the reader's or listener's mind, a rationally apprehended truth, a truth which, by virtue of its purely logical structure, would not otherwise move the audience nor arouse their passions. But Longinus's text never asserts a truth intended to become the object of a *persuasio*. In so far as it disregards the problem of truth, we could even consider it a sophistic treatise, but for the general character which in fact excludes this possibility.

But then, given that it constantly refers to poetry and metaphors, should we perhaps regard it as literary, as a treatise on 'style'? If so, what criteria of interpretation should we adopt in reading it?

The great philologist Augusto Rostagni set Longinus's work against the controversy which ensued among the followers of Apollodorus of Pergamum and Theodorus of Gadara.[17]

---

[17] *Del Sublime*, edited and translated by Augusto Rostagni (Milano: Istituto

Apollodorus of Pergamum was the advocate of rhetoric as a science and, therefore, a theoretician of rational discourse. Theodorus of Gadara, instead, regarded rhetoric as an art, and asserted the predominance of pathos in language. Rostagni saw Longinus's propositions as a sort of continuation of those pursued by Theodorus of Gadara.[18]

## 3) The Problem of Language: Logos as a Philosophical Question

The issues we are trying to resolve, and in light of which Longinus's text emerges in all of its significance, are directly connected to the manner in which the author's first definition of the sublime is interpreted. We must start with the Greek text: *Akrotes kai exoké tis logon estí ta ypse.*[19]

The latest translation by Giovanni Lombardo—to which I shall refer later[20]—gives *logos* as *style* (precisely in the interpretation of this term lies the key to our further development of the issues as we see them): "The sublime is the highest level of style."[21] On this point, this translation corresponds to the German one (which I consider the best, even though it is generally not known) by Renata von Scheliha, a member of Stephan George's circle.[22]

Russel, the author of the best and most detailed commentary on Longinus, translates *logos* not as *style* but as *discourse*, as Boileau had done before him.[23]

Why do I regard the translation of the term *logos* as central to the problems facing us? Because if we translate *logos* as style right from the start, we actually place the problem of sublime language in the realm of literature and style; we thus reduce Longinus's treatise to a literary work, which is what generally happens, and we do not see it

---

Editoriale Italiano, 1968).

[18] Nicholas of Cusa, xiiiff, especially xviii.

[19] *Del Sublime*, 1, 3.

[20] Pseudo Longino, *Il Sublime*, ed. G. Lombardo (Palermo: Aesthetica edizioni, 1987).

[21] *Il Sublime*, 1, 3, p. 29.

[22] Renata von Scheliha, *Die Schrift vam Erhabenen*, (Berlin: Kupper, 1939).

[23] Longinus, *On the Sublime*, ed. by D. A. Russel (Oxford: Clarendon, 1964); Boileau, *Traité du sublime ou du merveilleux dans le discours*, in *Oeuvres* (Paris: Librairie de Firmin-Didot et C., 1889), 367.

as a philosophical one. Let us bear in mind that the problem of style pertains to a particular type of language, and cannot be considered identical with the problem of the experience of the word, a much more originary, much more profound problem. From here we proceed to ask: What is the meaning of the connection between the sublime and language? Before giving his definition of the sublime, linking it to language, Longinus makes two important references.

First of all, in citing Caecilius of Calacte and the several examples of the sublime he offers in his works on the subject, he reproaches the author for failing to tell us "how we develop our nature to some degree of greatness."[24]

That leads us to the conclusion that the problem of the sublime, in its relation to the problem of language, is not a literary problem but a much more profound one, a problem which concerns the realization of the sublime found in human nature; this entails the primary manifestation of human nature in its highest structure, and this is not a literary issue, but an essentially philosophical one.

Secondly, human nature itself is not dealt with by Longinus in an abstract analysis of the issue; it is discussed within the limits of the *here* and *now* of its historical realization.

Addressing his friend Postumius Terentianus, Longinus asks his opinion on whether his work "may be thought useful to *public men.*"[25] Should we then regard the work *On the Sublime* and the problem of human nature (*physis*) as pertaining to rhetoric? If so, which rhetoric? Traditional rhetoric, perhaps, which aims at convincing us of a logical truth through persuasion?

Let us keep in mind that, in accordance with the arguments so far presented, reality cannot be identified by means of a rational process and cannot be expressed in the language that is peculiar to it; and if reality always manifests itself in an urgent appeal in the here and now, it is this historical language, bound to the here and now, it is this rhetorical language, in other words, which acquires original philosophical meaning.

The sublime, therefore, linked with the problem of language, can and should be legitimately dealt with not as abstract language, but as

---

[24] Russel, 1, 1.
[25] Russel, 1, 2.

historical language and, at the same time, as rhetorical language, though not in the traditional sense of the term. The treatise *On the Sublime* would, then, again acquire a completely new philosophical significance when compared to other treatments of language from traditional perspectives, metaphysical and logical.

Let us now focus on Longinus's second fundamental thesis, which follows his definition of the sublime as the highest form of language. Longinus asserts that the sublime "produces *ecstasy* rather than *persuasion* in the hearer,"[26] and emphasizes that 'ecstatic' language "is the source of the distinction of the very greatest poets and prose writers and the means by which they have given eternal glory to their own fame."[27] Must we then go back to the notion of an underivable language which is not purely 'literary,' and which 'distracts' us from our existential quests?

What is the difference between *persuasion* (*peithó*) and *ecstasy* (*ekstasis*)? Persuasion presupposes a logical truth, rationally provable, which, because of its structure, does not arouse our passions. Its metaphorical, illustrative, figurative nature concerns only passionateness. Its role in making the meaning of reality manifest is secondary; it is simply a 'means' to realize the rational truth already attained. 'Ecstatic' language, instead, is that which, in its originality, underivedness, and groundlessness—characteristics due to the fact that it is 'inexplicable'—does not have a *demonstrative*, but an *indicative* character. The text is specific on this point: "the combination of wonder and astonishment always proves superior to the merely persuasive and pleasant."[28]

At this point, we must draw the following conclusions from the theses just discussed. First of all, we are forced to exclude the possibility that the treatise *On the Sublime* is a rhetorical work in the traditional sense of the term, the sense in which rhetoric presupposes a logical truth to which it must further add a persuasive character unattainable through abstractions.

Secondly, the function of sublime language and its sphere of influence are not the rational, since rationality is based on logical

---

[26] Russel, 1, 4.
[27] Russel, 1, 3.
[28] Russel, 1, 4.

demonstrations and explanations which exclude moments of ecstasy and astonishment.

Thirdly, Longinus insists on the intimate connection between sublime language and originary *noesis*, that is the original awakening of reality: "Thought and expression are of course very much involved with each other."[29] This is the language to which "all orators and other writers" aspire; this is the language which "gives things life and makes them speak."[30] We have here before us the pre-eminence of the word which reveals over the word which explains, demonstrates, and rationalizes; it is the ungrounded word, which Longinus says is "the light that illuminates thought."[31]

Longinus's is a work illustrating the enlightening role of language grasped in its underivedness. The structure of sublime primordial language consists of the traits that make it dominant, compelling, wonderful, and astonishing.

Writing, then, raises issues which are neither literary, in a stylistic sense, nor traditionally rhetorical; these issues are different, even radically so, from the metaphysical conception of the function of language. Longinus deals with the sublime exclusively as it manifests itself in and through the word. The sublime is of the abyss and, therefore, still rationally undefinable. We can only speak of it in terms of language, of history, for these are what disclose our world to us in the temporal impetuosity of the sublime, which appears always different in the various instances of history. The author asserts that reality manifests itself in sublime language: hence, the challenging meaning of his original thesis.

> Nature made man to be no humble and lowly creature, but brought him into life and into the universe as into a great festival, to be both a spectator and an enthusiastic contestant in its competitions. She implanted in our minds from the start an irresistible desire for anything which is great and, in relation to ourselves, supernatural. The universe therefore is not wide enough for the range of human speculation and intellect. Our thoughts often travel beyond the boundaries of our surround-

---

[29] Russel, 30, 1.
[30] Ibid.
[31] Ibid.

ings. If anyone wants to know what we were born for, let him look round at life and contemplate the splendour, grandeur, and beauty in which it everywhere abounds.[32]

## 4) The Experience of Originary and Historical Reality in Sublime Language

The relevance of the treatise originates from the fact that it deals with language, not in order to define individual beings, but in order to assert the mystery of the word by identifying it with that of the sublime: the ungrounded structure of the word reveals the profound meaning of reality.

But from what can we derive the meaning of language if it does not depend on the logical determination of beings? Perhaps solely from the imagination of great poets and writers? Or is it possible to show that Longinus arrived at it by inverting the traditional method of philosophy in order to start with the underivable experience of the primordial character of language, which reveals rather than demonstrates?

In chapter eight he lists five sources for the experience of the sublime which directly depend on linguistic talents.[33] The first two are explicitly termed 'congenital' [Russel: natural] and are thus linked in an originary manner to the essence of human nature. The other three are technical, formal, and stylistic in nature: "the remaining three involve art."[34]

Of these five, we are interested in the first two. The first is defined as "the most important" and called "the power to conceive great thoughts";[35] the second, "strong and inspired emotion [*pathos*]."[36]

An initial question arises: How are we to interpret the statement that "these two sources are for the most part natural"?[37] I would tend to read in the term *authigenés* the meaning of 'born in its own place,' i.e., 'indigenous.' However, since it is difficult to see the link

---

[32] Russel, 35, 2-3.
[33] Russel, 8, 1.
[34] Ibid.
[35] Ibid.
[36] Ibid.
[37] Ibid.

between this meaning and the sublime, scholars have been translating it, as I have, with 'congenital,' that is 'innate'. We are so used by now to rational terminology when dealing with theoretical problems, that we would find unusual anything similar to the rendition I suggested. And yet, it is certainly not by chance that the author opted for a *metaphorical* term.

I would translate *authigenés* with 'aboriginal' in order to point to the underivedness of the source of the experience of the sublime. This experience has no place of origin; it is itself the place, the horizon, the origin which reveals primary reality in its impetuosity, which excludes any form of yearning for transcendental reality. The experience of sublime language is *determining of place and time in reality*.

We could even accept 'innate' or 'congenital,' but not in the sense that this source constitutes a faculty existing prior to our coming to be, and which must then be instilled in us. Here in-nate means that nature (understood as *phuein*, as birth and development) is the capacity of becoming manifest, as it appears in plants, animals and human language, revealing something completely new. As we read further in the text, the connection between *physis* and language will become clearer, and as it does, it will legitimate our stand that what we are dealing with is not merely an inclination toward the sublime. Longinus identifies this 'congenital' inclination toward the sublime primarily with *noesis*, as the faculty to conceive high thoughts, and specifies that it is "the first and the most important"[38] and, consequently, more primordial than a mere 'exuberant thrust' of the mind. This faculty of the human mind is an originary and projective apprehension, underivable and groundless, which reveals the sense (*noesis*) of reality in the experience of sublime language.

The impelling, dominant nature of the first source of elevated style becomes manifest through a second characteristic, the pathetic, which the author attributes to that same source. The author defines it as "strong and inspired emotion [*pathos*]."[39]

Let us keep in mind the kind of lexicon Longinus turns to when he speaks of this sublime passion: *enthousiastikón*, *enthousiazo*, *entheazo* are terms which point to the condition of one who is 'in-

---

[38] Ibid.
[39] Ibid.

spired,' to the state of one who is *éntheos*, who has within himself that which is sacred and integral. This sacredness, this divinity is deeply felt in the passionate experience of the noetic project of the word which discloses primordial knowledge. This sudden appearance of the sublime word can be identified with the metaphor of the ocean that Longinus uses to distinguish the Homer of the *Odyssey*, from the Homer of the *Iliad*. In the *Odyssey* he "no longer sustains the tension as it was in the tale of Troy"; we witness, instead, "greatness on the ebb. It is as though the Ocean were withdrawing into itself and flowing quietly in its own bed. Homer is lost in the realm of the fabulous and incredible."[40] As the ocean advances and withdraws, veiling and unveiling our beaches in high and low tides, so does the passion of sublime language cover and uncover reality, with a constant rhythm, which is that of historicity itself.

The author mentions the starting point of his discussion:

First then we must state where sublimity comes from: the orator must not have low or ignoble thoughts. Those whose thoughts and habits are trivial and servile all their lives cannot possibly produce anything admirable or worthy of eternity. Words will be great if thoughts are weighty.[41]

And the wave of this groundless passion bursts forth into sublime language, whose original violence Longinus exemplifies metaphorically by quoting verses from the Homeric text:

The imaginative pictures in the Battle of the Gods are also very remarkable:

And the great heavens and Olympus trumpeted
    around them.
Aidoneus, lord of the dead, was frightened in his
    depths;
and in fright he jumped from his throne, and shouted,
for fear the earth-shaker Poseidon might break
    through the ground,
and gods and men might see

---

[40] Russel, 9, 13.
[41] Russel, 9, 3.

the foul and terrible halls, which even the gods detest.

Do you see how the earth is torn from its foundations, Tartarus laid bare, and the whole universe
overthrown and broken up, so that all things—
Heaven and Hell, things mortal and things immor-
tal—share the warfare and the perils of that ancient
battle?[42]

We come now to a crucial question: Is the sacredness of original,
underivable, revealing language identified with a Platonic transcendence or is it identified with history? Longinus insists that language
is originally emotional and passionate in nature. Time is the goad of
what presses us on, drives us forward, becomes compelling, and is
made manifest in the instant yet to come, in the now, and in the
moment gone by of everchanging situations to whose binding force
we have to conform. The fundamental historicity of sublime language, its passion that is, manifests itself where the call appears and
becomes binding in the situational instant. It is only the need to
conform to that instant that unleashes passion, which then discloses
its own order in language. Those who believe to be exhibiting enthu-
siasm without being bound to the compelling force of the situation
are prey to a game of illusions: "They often fancy themselves possessed when they are merely playing the fool."[43] Unauthentic passion, we learn in chapter three, is that which does not correspond to
the right moment. True passion gives rise to unpremeditated words,
but words which come at the right moment (*kairós*).

The power and the rush of questions and answers occurring in
quick succession show how one can passionately experience a favor-
able moment: "For emotion [*pathos*] carries us away more easily when
it seems to be generated by the occasion rather than deliberately assumed
by the speaker, and the self-directed question and its answer represent
precisely this momentary quality of emotion [*pathos*]."[44]

Are we to conclude that *pathos* and *sublime language* are one and
the same? We do know that Longinus took Caecilius of Calacte to

---

[42] Russel, 9, 6; Homer, *Iliad*, 21, 388; 5, 750; 20, 60–65.
[43] Russel, 3, 2.
[44] Russel, 18, 2.

task for failing to speak of *pathos*: "I must first observe, however, that Caecilius has omitted ... emotion [*pathos*], for example. Now if he thought that sublimity and emotion [*pathos*] are one and the same thing and always existed and developed together, he was wrong. Some emotions, such as pity, grief, and fear, are found divorced from sublimity and with a low effect. Conversely, sublimity often occurs apart from emotion [*pathos*]."[45] The passions deemed lowly are those ontic in nature; as such, they are alien to the sublime. Sublime passion is ungrounded; it is not a passion accorded to individual beings, since it is precisely the passion of the abyss that reveals the everchanging meaning of individual beings in the various concrete situations in which they find themselves. Sublime passion, therefore, is not derivable from individual beings. It corresponds to the prophetic, evangelical word, the same word passionately experienced in the myths which mark the beginning of historical eras.

Because the sublime always manifests itself instantaneously, with lightning speed, it astonishes us; because it is inexplicable, it astounds us. It is through the sublime, and the benumbing astonishment it arouses in us, not through logical explanations, that we become aware of reality. Language which expresses and communicates the sublime is not an individual creation but a natural occurrence, a reality we are made to experience with passion: "It is our nature to be elevated and exalted by true sublimity. Filled with joy and pride, we come to believe we have created what we have only heard."[46]

True reality is not the reality of individual beings, but the reality of passion. It is not Platonic reality; it is, rather, the historicity of our world. Passion discloses reality, it raises the curtain on a play of which we are both the actors and the spectators. The power of nature manifests itself through, and subsists in, sublime language, pointing to its own ways and archetypes, sources of original images, places of the true sacredness of reality.

Longinus continuously refers to 'nature'. Nature, as the ungrounded manifestation of the sublime, follows its own method through which the sublime word discloses something 'new,' something fundamentally *human*: "Though nature is on the whole a law unto herself

---

[45] Russel, 8, 2.
[46] Russel, 7, 2.

in matters of emotion and elevation, she is not a random force and does not work altogether without method. She is herself in every instance a first and primary element of creation, but it is method that is competent to provide and contribute quantities and appropriate occasions for everything, as well as perfect correctness in training and application."[47] The author insists on the integration of nature with method or art: "Art is perfect when it looks like nature, nature is felicitous when it embraces concealed art."[48] Here, art, method, and rule are given the task of revealing the modalities of *kairós*, i.e., the proper occasion.

It is not at all, then, a question of inferring rules from poetry or lofty prose; it is a question of letting the originary, underivable, natural force of the sublime manifest itself at the right moment. "Most important of all, the very fact that some things in literature depend on nature alone can itself be learned only from art."[49] Study and method have precisely this function: to render the sublime communicable.

The present interpretation proves that Longinus's treatise retains its fundamentally philosophical validity. While traditional metaphysics, through the rational process, strives to identify nature with the multiplicity of individual beings, Longinus's point of departure is language as the manifestation of the power of mystery, of the abyss, and of the sublime. Every dualism of nature and spirit—that same dualism which traditional philosophy tried to overcome by asserting the pre-eminence of the rational process—thus ceases to exist. The mystery of language is no longer made manifest by the rational definition of individual beings; it is revealed through its function of initiating man into history. And here man must be interpreted as the being capable of the passionate experience of language.

Longinus's theses, then, as we have interpreted them, are still eminently valid today, a time when philosophy widely perceives as inadequate the rational definition of beings, the principle upon which Western thought is based. We must mention once again that it was Vico, the last great exponent of the humanist tradition, who, against

---

[47] Russel, 2, 2.
[48] Russel, 22, 1.
[49] Russel, 2, 3.

all forms of ontology, asserted the primordial character of poetic language. The poetic word is the originary form of language which marks the beginning of our historicity and allows for a 'clearing' to appear in the dark forest, the clearing which is the stage for our coming into humanity.

# The Experience of Time Past:
# M. Proust

## 1) The Dual Nature of Reality: The Urgent Appeal of Time

Our themes must now be examined more thoroughly. How? Again from a historical perspective with references to the historical development of philosophy? We have demonstrated elsewhere[1] that the uniqueness of Italian Humanism does not lie in its Christian reevaluation of Platonism and Neoplatonism, but rather on its discovery of the originary and underivable nature of language. We believe that in that work we have given adequate attention to the historical issue, to the exigencies of a historical hypothesis.

Our interest is now purely theoretical and we need to develop our thesis in view of the question of the originary function of language, which is closely related to poetry and to rhetoric in so far as it is the expression of the here and now of existence and of the urgent appeal of time. The awareness of this intimate relationship is present in the work of Marcel Proust,[2] a modern author generally studied, with few exceptions, only in a literary context. The fact that Proust has been accorded hardly any importance in the history of philosophy may provoke a negative reaction in our readers: it may seem absurd to refer to a writer of literary works in order to pursue our inquiries on a philosophical issue.

---

[1] E. Grassi, *Renaissance Humanism: Studies in Philosophy and Poetics*, Medieval & Renaissance Texts & Studies, vol. 51 (Binghamton, NY, 1988).
[2] M. Proust, *Remembrance of Things Past*, tr. C. K. Scott Moncrieff and T. Kilmartin (London: Chatto and Windus, 1981), 3 vols.

Let us keep in mind, however, that in every period of history authors get excluded or reevaluated, and that the term 'philosopher' is gradually given new and different meanings. In Renaissance Humanism, Poliziano did not consider himself a philosopher but insisted on being thought of as an 'interpreter,' taking, in this way, a polemical stance against what in his time was associated with a certain 'platonizing' philosophy. Still within the humanist tradition, Valla did not wish to be considered a philosopher, but a rhetorician, for he believed—going against the prevailing current of the times—that in rhetoric lay the foundations of an 'originary' philosophy. Finally, thanks to Descartes' new rationalism, the Latin authors as well as the Humanists, have hardly been granted the status of philosophers.

Taking into consideration these appraisals, we must reaffirm that the fundamental experience, on which Proust's work is grounded, is the passionate experience of the temporality of individual beings as well as the question of whether, through metaphorical language, we can finally experience a reality deeper than the reality of individual beings; in other words, whether it is possible to experience the 'sublime' Longinus had explored before him.

The basis of Proust's writings is the experience of the transient nature of individual beings, of their tragic continuous disappearance. Where, how and by what means can we conquer the flow of time and redeem individual beings by returning them to the realm of being, of that which is not transient but is and always exists?

In order to carry out this task, Proust writes a *phenomenology*, he describes an existential experience, not as Hegel had done—through the explanation of the dialectic process of rational thinking—but rather by shedding light on the reality of the abyss, an originary reality whose different appeals (of pleasure, of the need to escape from suffering, of anguish, of hope, of the compelling power of love) cause man to come into being in history by virtue of poetic language. Proust's phenomenology is therefore a phenomenology which purports to discover the flame that glows in the dark night of existence and reveals the meaning of the sorrow, joy and love we passionately experience in our lives. Proust radically rejects the notion that the individual beings we encounter in our daily lives correspond to an originary reality, and that their most profound meaning can be fathomed through logical, rational thinking.

Proust insists on the fundamental dual nature of reality. The first

type of reality concerns daily existence, it does not constitute originary reality: "...that life of ours which cannot effectually observe
itself and of which the observable manifestations need to be translated
and, often, to be read backwards and laboriously deciphered. [...] it
is the task of art to undo this work of theirs, making us travel back
in the direction from which we have come to the depths where what
has really existed lies unknown within us."[3]

The second is originary reality, the reality of the abyss: "One feels,
yes, but what one feels is like a negative which shows only blackness
until one has placed it near a special lamp and which must also be
looked at in reverse. [...] Then only ... does one distinguish, and
with what difficulty, the lineaments of what one felt."[4]

If we remain attached to individual beings for the purpose of identifying them rationally, we lose ourselves in a false and illusory knowledge
in no way related to the experience of the true, originary being, a
knowledge which "in that flight to get away from our own life (which
we have not the courage to look at) ... goes by the name of erudi-
tion."[5] It is therefore a matter of distinguishing between knowledge of
individual beings and knowledge of being: "Since every impression is
double and the one half which is sheathed in the object is prolonged in
ourselves by another half which we alone can know, we speedily find
means to neglect this second half, which is the one on which we
ought to concentrate, and to pay attention only to the first half."[6]

Proust's tale, his myth, is the story of the discovery of the abyss:
it is the wearisome raising of the curtain that discloses the real spectacle of humanity. His story emphasizes primarily the anguished
evocation of the originary appeal: "to find that first image again, even
though I am no longer the 'I' who first beheld it, even though I must
make way for the 'I' that I then was if that 'I' summons the thing
that it once knew and that the 'I' of to-day does not know."[7]

Proust describes with great precision the experience of the appeals
of the abyss which determine man's existence—the evocation of the

---

[3] *Remembrance of Things Past*, 3:932.
[4] *Remembrance of Things Past*, 3:933.
[5] *Remembrance of Things Past*, 3:927.
[6] *Remembrance of Things Past*, 3:927.
[7] *Remembrance of Things Past*, 3:923.

past, the unveiling of the past to recover it, and the redemption of the past, which is more than its mere repetition, but constitutes, rather, the quest for a deeper reality, a 'new truth':

> And then, after I had dwelt for some little time upon these resurrections of the memory, the thought came to me that in another fashion certain obscure impressions ... had solicited my attention in a fashion somewhat similar to these reminiscences, except that they concealed within them not a sensation dating from an earlier time, but a new truth.[8]

Proust stated that originary reality, unveiled with such great efforts, warrants the efforts themselves, "efforts of the same kind as those that we make to recall something that we have forgotten, as if our finest ideas were like tunes which, as it were, come back to us although we have never heard them before and which we have to make an effort to hear and to transcribe."[9] The question of time is vital to this experience, and for Proust it corresponds to a power which dominates individual beings and subjects them to an unyielding process of transformation, to a metamorphosis that disallows for their reduction to abstract, logical entities. By virtue of his creativity, man is usually able to effect this transformation—the metamorphosis of beings. In the experience of time, however, he becomes aware that the transformations in places, institutions and individuals occur independently of his own activity. The world of men presents itself as a world of "puppets bathed in the immaterial colours of the years, puppets which exteriorised Time, Time which by Habit is made invisible and to become visible seeks bodies, which whenever it finds it seizes, to display its magic lantern upon them."[10]

Hence the anguish of the individual who encounters someone who has aged, who sees a building eroded by time, or a wilted flower. The experience of time past overwhelms him, even in spite of his intentions to decipher its message: "I had made the discovery of this destructive action of Time at the very moment when I had conceived the ambition to make visible, to intellectualise in a work of art,

---

[8] *Remembrance of Things Past,* 3:911–912.
[9] *Remembrance of Things Past,* 3:912.
[10] *Remembrance of Things Past,* 3:964.

realities that were outside Time."[11] Time constantly places before our eyes the process of metamorphosis, the non-originary character of individual beings. It is impossible to escape the violence of time, which compels us to ask ourselves whether in the continuous meta-morphosis of reality we can reach an originary world that exists paradoxically, as a contradiction, a mystery that cannot be expressed by rational language.

Proust formulates the problem in the following manner:

> For to 'recognise' someone, and, *a fortiori*, to learn someone's identity after having failed to recognise him, is to predicate two contradictory things of a single subject, it is to admit that what was here, the person whom one remembers, no longer exists, and also that what is now here is a person whom one did not know to exist; and to do this we have to apprehend a mystery almost as disturbing as that of death."[12]

Time devours things, individuals, names, places: "Time in which, as in some transforming fluid, men and societies and nations are immersed."[13] The recovery of time past, or 'lost,' is thus identified existentially with the question of 'remembrance' and of memory, of the passionately experienced appeal of the abyss. New problems always arise independently of rational and intellectual thought. Philosophy is born of the experience of the metamorphic and meta-phorical nature of individual beings and is the expression of the passionate experience, in the here and now of history, of the appeal of the abyss. This is the philosophy that is born of a story, of a tale, such as Erasmus's in *The Praise of Folly*, Leon Battista Alberti's in *Momus*, Vives's in *Fabula de homine*.[14] It is also a philosophy that desecrates the appeal of the abyss, referred to by Meister Eckhart in his sermons when he demythologizes the 'dark light' experienced by St. John of the Cross or the meaning of Saint Theresa of Avila's dialogues with her divine lover.

---

[11] *Remembrance of Things Past*, 3:971.

[12] *Remembrance of Things Past*, 3:982.

[13] *Remembrance of Things Past*, 3:974.

[14] Cf. *Renaissance Humanism: Studies in Philosophy and Poetics*; E. Grassi and Lorch, *Folly and Insanity in Renaissance Literature*, Medieval & Renaissance Texts & Studies, vol. 42 (Binghamton, 1986).

We are confronted here with the question of being and time, not of time and individual beings. Proust accomplishes his task gradually: firstly, by describing the process of becoming of individual beings and the concomitant loss of time on the part of those who remain desperately attached to them; secondly, by criticizing those who claim to grasp the essence of reality through rationality; thirdly, by asserting that the power of the abyss manifests itself through passions, principally through erotic passion and through the experience of sorrow. Finally, he demonstrates that the power of the abyss becomes manifest in ineffable, underived moments which are themselves ephemeral.

The experience of time constitutes the mystery of reality in so far as it returns us to the compelling force within it, the compelling force whose *parousia* is not a rationally deducible occurrence: a pure 'event'.

## 2) A Critique of Rationality: The Realm of Passions

We will refer to Proust's work to illustrate, once again, what philosophy calls the ontological difference between being and beings. It is surprising that Proust always discusses it in terms of life experience, never as a theoretical issue. The 'spectacle,' the drama, the play of this difference is not only seen by the author, it is also experienced by him passionately and endured painfully, as it presents itself on the stage of the theater of our world. Only by experiencing passions, themselves indicative signs, can we arrive at the foundations of individual beings, because it is precisely through them, in the experience of pain and pleasure, of fear and hope, of love and hate, that the mystery—the abyss—reveals itself.

Hence Proust's first task is to emphasize the value of what is revealed to us through our senses and to accord proper significance to the passions aroused in us by our sensory experience. The pain and pleasure aroused by the senses are not subjective; they provide us with the text of a reality which we ourselves have not written, but which we must read and interpret: "The book whose hieroglyphs are patterns not traced by us is the only book that really belongs to us. [...] Only the impression ... is a criterion of truth [...]. The impression is for the writer what experiment if for the scientist."[15]

---

[15] *Remembrance of Things Past*, 3:914.

Here we have again the theme on which Lorenzo Valla based his philosophy in his *De voluptate*: "that pure substance of ourselves that is a past impression ... does not present itself to our memory except in the midst of sensations which suppress it."[16] Usually, we interpret passions as sensory reactions to the external world and we consider the external world the cause of all passions. But for something to appear to us, painful or pleasurable, there must be something else which 'opens up' for us the possibility of these alternatives. Sensory perceptions are signs whose meaning must be interpreted: "The task was to interpret the given sensations as signs of so many laws and ideas, by trying to think—that is to say, to draw forth from the shadow—what I had merely felt, by trying to convert it into its spiritual equivalent."[17]

The reading of the sacred and mysterious signs of individual beings for the purpose of understanding their essence, is basically a personal one: "What we have not had to decipher, to elucidate by our own efforts, what was clear before we looked at it, is not ours. From ourselves comes only that which we drag forth from the obscurity which lies within us, that which to others is unknown."[18]

Proust's phenomenology of passions—"appetite, anger, fear, confidence, envy, joy, love, hatred, longing emulation, pity"[19]—does not have the same goals as Aristotle had set for himself in his *Nicomachean Ethics*.[20] In Plato's *Phaedrus*, Lysias had used a similar type of argument in order to invalidate erotic passion. Proust's intention is to do exactly the opposite. Passion invests individual beings with an unexpected intensity, which brings about a transformation that institutes new relationships: "A sort of nervous system, a sensory network which ramified into each of its rooms and sent a constant stimulus to his heart."[21] We are in a sphere completely unrelated to

---

[16] M. Proust, *Against Sainte-Beuve and Other Essays*, tr. J. Sturrock (Harmondsworth: Penguin, 1988), 4–5.

[17] *Remembrance of Things Past*, 3:912.

[18] *Remembrance of Things Past*, 3:914.

[19] Aristotle, *Nicomachean Ethics*, tr. W. D. Ross, revised by S. O. Urmson, in *The Complete Works of Aristotle*, the revised Oxford translation, ed. J. Barnes (Princeton, NJ: Princeton Univ. Press, 1984) 1105 b 21.

[20] 1105 b 21 and book 5.

[21] *Remembrance of Things Past*, 1:247.

abstract reality: "He was well aware that his love was something that
did not correspond to anything outside itself, verifiable by others
besides him."[22] Passion is not a psychological phenomenon; its
depiction becomes the attempt to hear the stormy mystery of the
originary appeal in the sound of a seashell. Hence the need to emphasize the elements of passion, not to undermine their importance: the
colouring of the skin, the characteristics of a face, the timbre of a
voice, the sudden gleam of the eyes in the surreal light of passion and
the compelling presence of the radiant body that fascinates us and
that lives in the touch of a hand, in the fold of a dress, in the sculpted
shape of a knee. Metamorphosis occurs through passion. It is in the
realm of passion that we must search for and read the "illegible and
divine traces":[23] "it almost seems as though a writer's works, like
the water in an artesian well, mount to a height which is in propor-
tion to the depth to which suffering has penetrated his heart."[24]

Passionateness reveals itself as reality because the choice of pleasure
or pain constitutes the charge of objectivity. Proust's story unravels
in the midst of passions, in the forest of originary reality, as it discloses its own progress and its characters, its settings, its encounters and
separations: "We are, as it were, posted at a window, badly placed
but looking out over an expanse of sea, and only during a storm,
when our thoughts are agitated by perpetually changing movements,
do they elevate to a level at which we can see it, the whole law-
governed immensity which normally, when the calm weather of
happiness leaves it smooth, lies beneath our line of vision."[25]

Rationality is but the illusion of our identification with reality
which hides the transformation of individual beings until its outer
covering breaks open to expose the fruit, the true reality that empow-
ers all passions. The distinction between being and beings appears to
us in the very flash of this experience: "When I saw an external
object, my consciousness that I was seeing it would remain between
me and it, surrounding it with a thin spiritual border that prevented
me from ever touching its substance directly; for it would somehow

---

[22] *Remembrance of Things Past*, 1:259.
[23] *Remembrance of Things Past*, 1:304.
[24] *Remembrance of Things Past*, 3:946.
[25] *Remembrance of Things Past*, 3:933.

evaporate before I could make contact with it, just as an incandescent body that is brought into proximity with something wet never actually touches its moisture, since it is always preceded by a zone of evaporation."[26] The incandescence of the object, namely, the identity and nonidentity of the individual beings, displaces things, places, relationships: "Next to this central belief which, while I was reading, would be constantly reaching out from my inner self to the outer world, towards the discovery of Truth, came the emotions around in me by the action in which I was taking part, for these afternoons were crammed with more dramatic events than occur, often, in a whole lifetime."[27]

The rational idea reveals itself as a prefabricated being, a being rationally distilled and 'abstracted' from time, from place and from passions. This is an nonexistent world because: "'None of us can be said to constitute a material whole, which is identical for everyone, and need only be turned up like a page in an account-book or the record of a will.'"[28] Proust's work constitutes a coherent attempt to redeem reality through a nonrational process: "Daily, I attach less value to the intellect. Daily, I realize more clearly that only away from it can the writer repossess something of our past impressions."[29] Rationality abstracts reality from the tension in which beings emerge: "...his intelligence had not embodied in them anything of the past save fictitious extracts which preserved none of the reality."[30] Proust insists on and makes a radical distinction between truths grasped through our intellect and truths that are mediated by the senses: "For the truths which the intellect apprehends directly in the world of full and unimpeded light have something less profound, less necessary than those which life communicates to us against our will in an impression which is material because it enters us through the senses but yet has a spiritual meaning which it is possible for us to extract."[31]

Proust demonstrates that the rational process cannot grasp the metamorphic structure of individual beings, and that it cannot reveal

---

[26] *Remembrance of Things Past,* 3:90.
[27] *Remembrance of Things Past,* 1:91.
[28] *Remembrance of Things Past,* 1:20.
[29] *Against Sainte-Beuve,* 3.
[30] *Remembrance of Things Past,* 1:376.
[31] *Remembrance of Things Past,* 3:912.

their identity and nonidentity. As a matter of fact, such a process conceals it all. It is futile to begin our quest for reality with institutionalized scientific preconceptions or with mundane ambitions. He has no faith in an individual who feels deference "towards mediocre writers in order to succeed, shortly, in becoming an Academician, when the Academy and the Faubourg Saint-Germain have no more to do with that part of the Eternal Mind ... than with the law of causality or the idea of God."[32] Proust searches for the essence of things but confesses: "Experience had taught me only too well the impossibility of attaining in the real world to what lay deep within myself ... disappointed as I had always been by the actuality of places and people."[33]

The distinction between being and beings is decisive for our author. Our process of identification of things may begin with rational premises but it will lead us to nothing new if it remains rational. Thinking is concerned with making decisions and drawing conclusions from what has been already discovered, but invention is not logical; it is ingenious. It unveils individual beings and discloses their meaning as metaphors of being, which makes itself manifest and compels in the everchanging moments of history.

Hence the problem: How do we arrive at the essence of things? "To this contemplation of the essence of things I had decided therefore that in the future I must attach myself, so as somehow to immobilise it. But how, by what means, was I to do this?"[34]

## 3) Memory and the Abyss

It may seem absurd. In the history of Western thought, Meister Eckhart proclaimed the importance of the ontological difference, thereby preparing the way for a renewed religious spirit, which, however, was soon reduced to a sterile and exclusively dogmatic proclamation of the Christian faith. Eckhart had identified the appeal of the abyss, in whose realm the most profound meaning of individual beings manifests itself as the Word of God. Heidegger desecrated that Word. Proust, while demythologizing the appeal of the abyss, makes a concerted effort to point out the essentially metaphoric and

---

[32] *Remembrance of Things Past,* 1:600.
[33] *Remembrance of Things Past,* 3:910.
[34] *Remembrance of Things Past,* 3:909.

metamorphic character of all that becomes manifest. He points to a metaphysics of reality which prescribes the thesis of the primacy and of the primordial nature of poetic language.

We now ask ourselves the following question: After all our considerations, have we managed to redeem what time destroys and what, according to Proust's formula, "would be to secure a contact with the Beyond"?[35]

Sensory perceptions are signs that must be deciphered: ". . . truth will be attained by him only when he takes two different objects, states the connexion between them—a connexion analogous in the world of art to the unique connexion which in the world of science is provided by the law of causality—and encloses them in the memory links of a well-wrought style; truth—and life too—can be attained by us only when, by comparing a quality common to two sensations, we succeed in extracting their common essence and in reuniting them to each other, liberated from the contingencies of time, within a metaphor."[36]

Style emerges from the revelation of the difference between being and beings. The meaning of individual beings resides in the investigation of passions in whose realm they appear:

> Then, quite independently of all these literary preoccupations and in no way connected with them, suddenly a roof, a gleam of sunlight on a stone, the smell of a path would make me stop still to enjoy the special pleasure that each of them gave me, and also because they appeared to be concealing beyond what my eyes could see, something which they invited me to come and take but which despite all my efforts I never managed to discover. Since I felt that this something was to be found in them, I would stand there motionless. . . . I would concentrate on recalling exactly the line of the roof, the colour of the stone, which, without my being able to understand why, had seemed to me to be bursting, ready to open, to yield up to me the secret treasure of which they were themselves no more than lids.[37]

---

[35] *Remembrance of Things Past*, 1:52.

[36] *Remembrance of Things Past*, 3:924–925.

[37] *Remembrance of Things Past*, 1:194–195.

Proust works out the phenomenology of the experience of ontological difference with great precision. He first experiences the identity of individual beings knowing, however, that something essential
escapes him: "I looked at the three trees; I could see them plainly,
but my mind felt that they were concealing something which it could
not grasp."[38] Already he suspects that there is something else operat-
ing behind this. This otherness does not correspond to the individual
beings themselves, but it is precisely in the concealment of their
identity and difference that Proust feels the joy of the experience of
an appeal that goes beyond the image itself:

> I recognised that kind of pleasure which requires, it is true, a
> certain effort on the part of the mind... That pleasure, the
> object of which I could only dimly feel, which I must create
> for myself, I experienced only on rare occasions, but on each of
> these it seemed to me that the things that had happened in the
> meantime were of little importance, and that in attaching
> myself to the reality of that pleasure alone could I at length
> begin to lead a true life.[39]

Proust is first astonished by this experience ("I sat there thinking
of nothing") and then turns inwards to an interior landscape where
the individual being can be seen ("then with my thoughts collected,
compressed and strengthened I sprang further forward in the direction
of the trees, or rather in that inner direction at the end of which I could
see them inside myself"[40]) and where the meaning of the individual
being comes forth as if emerging from a remote, almost unidentifiable
past ("a meaning as obscure, as hard to grasp, as is a distant past"[41]).
   The compelling force ("And meanwhile they were coming towards me; perhaps some fabulous apparition, a ring of witches or of
Norns would propound their oracles to me"[42]) appears on a peak
between being and beings and obliges Proust to confront the issue of
the abyss:

---

[38] *Remembrance of Things Past*, 1:771.
[39] *Remembrance of Things Past*, 1:771.
[40] *Remembrance of Things Past*, 1:771–772.
[41] *Remembrance of Things Past*, 1:772.
[42] *Remembrance of Things Past*, 1:772–773.

For a moment it [Gilberte's signature] merely gave an impression of unreality to everything around me. With dizzy speed the improbable signature danced about my bed, the fireplace, the four walls. I saw everything reel, as one does when one falls from a horse, and I asked myself whether there was not an existence altogether different from the one I knew, in direct contradiction of it, but itself the real one.[43]

For Proust it is a matter of evoking, of retrieving from the darkness the most profound of realities: "Like ghosts they seemed to be appealing to me to take them with me, to bring them back to life."[44] What emerges from the abyss manifests itself as the only truth which gives us happiness, the truth that reveals itself as the epicenter, not only of a literary work, but of our life: "It was bearing me away from what alone I believed to be true, what would have made me truly happy."[45]

In this experience man emerges to Proust as a Prometheus chained to the rock of beings, vulnerable to the beckoning songs of the Oceanides.[46] This is the call Proust acknowledges as the essence of life "more than an aesthetic feeling, a fleeting but exalted ambition to stay and live there forever."[47] Writing, then, requires a style that has nothing to do with literary perfection but is rather "the revelation, which by direct and conscious methods would be impossible, of the qualitative difference, the uniqueness of the fashion in which the world appears to each one of us, a difference which, if there were no art, would remain for ever the secret of every individual."[48]

Proust, moreover, insists relentlessly on the inadequacies of material pleasure, which is the result of our attachment to individual beings and which he juxtaposes to the pleasure which derives from that which is beyond time, experienced in the instantaneousness of the here and now of existence. He speaks therefore of "Impressions [that] ... could not but vanish at the touch of a direct enjoyment

---

[43] *Remembrance of Things Past*, 1:538–539.
[44] *Remembrance of Things Past*, 1:773.
[45] *Remembrance of Things Past*, 1:773.
[46] *Remembrance of Things Past*, 1:774.
[47] *Remembrance of Things Past*, 1:775.
[48] *Remembrance of Things Past*, 3:431–432.

which had been powerless to engender them,"[49] as we experience the precariousness of sexual pleasure, "the act of physical possession (in which, paradoxically, the possessor possesses nothing)."[50]

There is here a distinction between two types of pleasure: an 'originary,' primordial pleasure, wherein beings are revealed as a metaphor requiring no explanation, and an unstable kind of pleasure which depends on their transience and which cannot be fixed nor truly possessed. "... a cool, fusty smell which ... filled me with a pleasure of a different kind from other pleasures, which leaves one more unstable, incapable of grasping them, of possessing them, a pleasure that was solid and consistent, on which I could lean for support, delicious, soothing, rich with a truth that was lasting, unexplained and sure."[51] Proust points constantly to the experience of this ontological difference: "But even apart from rare moments such as these, in which suddenly we feel the original entity quiver and resume its form, carve itself out of syllables now dead ..."[52] Such an experience has "the violence of my exaltation,"[53] the intoxication provoked by pure disclosure, and the inebriation of pure appearance: "... inebriation brings about for an hour or two a state of subjective idealism, pure phenomenalism; everything is reduced to appearances."[54] And he insists on the brevity of these extratemporal moments and on the moments themselves: "Unfortunately the coefficient which thus alters our values alters them only during that hour of intoxication. The people who were no longer of any importance, whom we scattered with our breath like soap-bubbles, will to-morrow resume their density."[55]

In the context of this experience, sorrow acquires the significant function of revealing the expression of the transience of individual beings: perhaps only geniuses have no need for this experience to attain the knowledge of the distinction between being and beings:

---

[49] *Remembrance of Things Past,* 3:911.
[50] *Remembrance of Things Past,* 1:255.
[51] *Remembrance of Things Past,* 1:530.
[52] *Remembrance of Things Past,* 2:6.
[53] *Remembrance of Things Past,* 1:874.
[54] *Remembrance of Things Past,* 1:874.
[55] *Remembrance of Things Past,* 1:874.

"... the whole art of living is to make use of the individuals through whom we suffer ..."[56]

We will try to better illustrate the essence of the ontological difference by interpreting the episode of Vinteuil's musical phrase. Making music presupposes the use of an instrument that must be previously tuned. If the instrument is a piano we rely on a tuner: his job is to regulate the instrument in accordance with the laws of musical harmony, namely, in accordance with the ordered system of high and low tones outside of which playing is not possible. Generally speaking, a European tuner will not be able to tune an oriental instrument, for he is not acquainted with the laws of musical harmony that belong to another world. Proust states, consequently, that musicians, by playing on their instruments, conjure up 'worlds': "... a few great artists ... when they awaken in us the emotion corresponding to the theme they have discovered, ... [show us] what richness, what variety lies hidden, unknown to us, in that vast, unfathomed and forbidding night of our soul which we take to be an impenetrable void."[57]

It is therefore in the context of this ordered system—not arbitrary, not subjective, but rooted in the passions evoked by sounds—that the musician, by playing, reveals his world. Based on this, Proust makes a distinction between "a miserable stave of seven notes"[58] and what he calls "an immeasurable keyboard (still almost entirely unknown) on which, here and there only, separated by the thick darkness of its unexplored tracts, some few among the millions of keys of tenderness, of passion, of courage, of serenity, which compose it, each one different from all the rest as one universe differs from another, have been discovered by a few great artists."[59]

Vinteuil's musical phrase, which affects Swann so profoundly, stresses the following points: 1) an instrument is an instrument only if it is tuned according to the rules of the 'musical game,' namely, to the principles of duration, rhythm and pitch variations, melodiousness of sounds; 2) what is revealed in a musical performance can be

---

[56] *Remembrance of Things Past*, 3:935.
[57] *Remembrance of Things Past*, 1:380.
[58] *Remembrance of Things Past*, 1:380.
[59] *Remembrance of Things Past*, 1:380.

revealed only if the instrument is the 'organ' of an originary order; 3) the essential elements of music are not the sounds themselves, in so far as they are acoustic phenomena, but the fact that they are tuned in accordance with a system which varies with time and place; 4) not only are there different musical worlds—European, Oriental, African, etc.—but each musician, with his tuned instrument, executes in the context of the system, his own 'performance' and reveals his own world; 5) the great mystery is the very 'gift' of these ordered systems wherein the different performances—including the performance of our own life—can be realized; 6) only in the realm of such a system can the musicality of the individual musician be disclosed and the single musical scores be executed well or poorly, as the case may be.

These considerations point to the distinction between sounds and musical system and to the difference between individual beings and being. It is indeed a radical difference that cannot be denied, as we cannot "doubt the luminosity of a lamp that has just been lit, in view of the changed aspect of everything in the room."[60] For Proust there is perhaps a meager consolation: "Perhaps it is not-being that is the true state, and all our dream of life is inexistent; but, if so, we feel that these phrases of music, these conceptions which exist in relation to our dream, must be nothing either. We shall perish, but we have as hostages these divine captives who will follow and share our fate. And death in their company is somehow less bitter, less inglorious, perhaps even less probable."[61]

In music—as ultimately in all human games—the rules are not deducible and, like myths, they touch us, dominate us and rush over us in quick succession. We will never fathom the code, the rules that govern the games if we base our reflection merely on the sounds themselves, on colors, dice, cards.

In turn, the rules of the game of existence are not set up by man, but become manifest in the very process of the playing of the game. The experience of the ontological difference enables us to begin our journey, to move, to play a part, to speak with great precision: "never was spoken language so inexorably determined, never had it

---

[60] *Remembrance of Things Past*, 1:381.
[61] *Remembrance of Things Past*, 1:381.

known questions so pertinent, such irrefutable replies."[62] Proust's
statement on the difference between originary being and individual
beings is a valid one not only in the context of one particular aspect
of reality, such as literature, for example, but in all contexts of our
existence:

> The greatness ... of true art ... lay, I had come to see, else-
> where: we have to rediscover, to reapprehend, to make our-
> selves fully aware of that reality, remote from our daily preoc-
> cupations ... that reality which it is very easy for us to die
> without ever having known and which is, quite simply, our
> life. Real life, life at last laid bare and illuminated ... is litera-
> ture.[63]

Proust identifies the disclosure of originary reality with the demy-
thologized experience of a joy that transcends the boundaries of
individual beings and that emerges on the vertiginous peak of the
awareness of the inherent duality of reality.

Only by virtue of the experience of such transcendence can we
free ourselves from our subjective world through an instantaneous
vision, inadmissible and illegitimate within a rational context. Consequently, what Proust defines as a work of art must not be understood
as a reproduction of an attachment to beings: "and this lie is all that
can be reproduced by the art that styles itself 'true to life.' ... a mere
vain and tedious duplication of what our eyes see and our intellect
records."[64]

The revelation of what transcends individual beings and is simultaneously immanent in them, which constitutes the response to the
appeals of the abyss, acquires the dramatic force of a "true last judg-
ment."[65] We must seek "something that is different from them,"[66]
we must probe deeper into their meaning: "...we feel so strongly
during the hours in which we are at work that the individual whom
we love is being dissolved into a vaster reality that at moments we

---

[62] *Remembrance of Things Past,* 1:382.
[63] *Remembrance of Things Past,* 3:931.
[64] *Remembrance of Things Past,* 3:931.
[65] *Remembrance of Things Past,* 3:914.
[66] *Remembrance of Things Past,* 3:932.

succeed in forgetting her and we come to suffer [no longer] from our love. . ."[67]

And so Proust finally writes with great precision about the structure of originary memory. It is not a doubling of individual beings, so to speak, but the revelation of the originary appeal through experienced sensations: "No, it was no mere analogous sensation nor even a mere echo or replica of a past sensation."[68] Time and place belonging to the past coincide with the present: It is a resurrection within the contradiction of the simultaneity of past and present ("in a dazed uncertainty such as we feel sometimes [. . .] Fragments of existence withdrawn from Time"[69]), fragments belonging to eternity, yet fleeting ("but the contemplation, though it was of eternity, had been fugitive"[70]).

The authenticity of experience is revealed, for Proust, though the objective impossibilities of its rational deliverance.

## 4) Problems

The 'unbridled' imagination is an overwhelming force and Proust's words, unmediated by thought, but passionately experienced, never cease to astonish us. Imagine the prow of a ship: before us the expanse of the sea and the stillness of an island; in the breeze, the purple plumbagos, the bleeding bougainvilleas, the steel-gray agaves. Why, given the transience of beings, do we feel not only the desire but the pressing need to express ourselves? Proust's answer to this question is the following: "One sees oneself as no more than the trustee, who may depart at any moment, of intellectual secrets which depart with one."[71] This is reaffirmed in answer to the demand of the dead for their redemption: "I felt myself enhanced by this work which I bore within me as by something fragile and precious which had been entrusted to me and which I should have liked to deliver intact into the hands of those for whom it was intended, hands which

---

[67] *Remembrance of Things Past,* 3:942.
[68] *Remembrance of Things Past,* 3:907.
[69] *Remembrance of Things Past,* 3:908.
[70] *Remembrance of Things Past,* 3:908.
[71] *Against Sainte-Beuve,* 10.

were not my own."[72] And again: "Yet it was precisely when the thought of death had become a matter of indifference to me that I was beginning once more to fear death, under another form, it is true, as a threat not to myself but to my book."[73]

Light, colors, the cool breezes, evoke the passions whose absence causes beings to freeze in an abstract reality. We seek in the brilliance of the light, in the rustling of leaves, in a flower, the confirmation, the compelling forces of life, and yet we hear in them the anguished echoes of the call of the dead. It is the rejection of all consolation. To seek it would mean to express our inability to resist the tension that dislocates the junctures of our vitality. I would be anguished "at turning my back for ever on a past I would never see again, at denying the dead who were holding tender, impotent arms to me and seemed to be saying 'Resurrect us.' "[74]

By following the path traced for us by Proust, we gain an insight, we have a vision: Is it a tragic one? "The idea of Time ... it was a spur, it told me that it was time to begin if I wished to attain to what I had sometimes perceived in the course of my life, in brief lightning-flashes."[75]

Is it truly ridiculous to cling desperately to our past? The very breath of life obliges us to continue to plow the waves under a starless sky, with no constellation to guide us, in the darkness of the night where an expression of tenderness, the fear of sorrow, the anticipation of joy—indeed all passions!—thrust our ship forward and seem to point to new paths. But in reality, the only sign that we are moving at all is the mysterious murmuring sound of the waters below. And we hear the constant echo of the anguished cry: "Phantoms of a past dear to me, so dear that my heart was beating fit to break, they held impotent arms out to me, like the shades whom Aeneas met in the underworld."[76] In the luminous waves, in these waves of colors and scents, in this forest of everchanging metamorphoses, the enchantment of metaphors shines bright with all its

---

[72] *Remembrance of Things Past,* 3:1093.
[73] *Remembrance of Things Past,* 3:1095.
[74] *Against Sainte-Beuve,* 6–7.
[75] *Remembrance of Things Past,* 3:1088.
[76] *Against Sainte-Beuve,* 6.

seductive power. Our awareness of this validates once more our existence and arouses in us feelings of shame because, in reality, we are unable to see any shore to anchor at, as we are blinded by the light, the glare of the waters and the awareness of the destructive power of time.

Throughout life, we are accompanied by two guardian angels: anguish and hope. With them we engage in the uninterrupted dialogue of existence.

> But when from a long-distant past nothing subsists, after the people are dead, after the things are broken and scattered, taste and smell alone, more fragile but more enduring, more unsubstantial, more persistent, more faithful, remain poised a long time, like souls, remembering, waiting, hoping, amid the ruins of all the rest; and bear unflinchingly, in the tiny and almost impalpable drop of this essence, the vast structure of recollection.[77]

Must we then exorcise reality only to remain suspended for an instant over the chasm of extratemporality? By tracing in a daily effort the limits of our work, by refining and perfecting it, by exploring through our work the depths of the reality of our existence, we sketch the contours of our own grave: "The writer feeds his book, he strengthens the parts of it which are weak, he protects it, but afterwards it is the book that grows, that designates its author's tomb and defends it against the world's clamour and for a while against oblivion."[78]

Should we protect our work against the sweeping forces of oblivion? Yes, but unlike authors such as Ovid and Horace, without faith in eternal remembrance. Our awareness of the destructive, metamorphic power of time is warranted by the dust overflowing in museums. The revelation of the most profound reality occurs through *praxis*, not through *poiesis*, which is merely subjective creation. For this reason, what is revealed to us has a beginning, an existence and an end, and our work fades in the darkness of time past like the diamond whose crystallized brilliance is hidden in the ground, concealed by earthy layers of darkness.

---

[77] *Remembrance of Things Past*, 1:50–51.
[78] *Remembrance of Things Past*, 1:1089.

In writing about his own work, Proust states that he wishes "to endure his book like a form of fatigue, to accept it like a discipline, build it up like a church, follow it like a medical regime."[79] Such a work must decipher the hieroglyphics of passions inscribed in all human beings and reveal their secret by examining and magnifying them as the optician does with his lens: "For it seemed to me that they would not be 'my' readers but the readers of their own selves, my book being merely a sort of magnifying glass like those which the optician at Combray used to offer his customers—it would be my book, but with its help I would furnish them with the means of reading what lay inside themselves."[80]

If such is our task, then we cannot allow ourselves to find a false sense of security in the rational definition of reality. We must search for it in the realm of paradox, in the realm of nonreason, wherein the 'unheard' appears on the scene of history. Before such a spectacle we will be overcome with astonishment and anguish as we witness a continuing destruction, the disappearance of the protagonists who played their role fully aware of their own death. Is all this tragedy or comedy? Or is it both simultaneously?

Inherent in passions is the appeal of the abyss that weaves in the here and now of history its tapestry of images, people, places and times. We want to save the tapestry, snatch it from the jaws of death by remaining faithful to it. But how? With our will, our compassion? The temporal transience of a beloved, the awareness of her birth, life, thoughts, the tragic experience of her death, all these imply not only the disappearance of the beloved from the world, but also the transformation of the lover: "The self that had loved her, which another self had already almost entirely supplanted, would reappear, stimulated far more often by a trivial than by an important event."[81]

In the realm of passion—be it hope, anguish, or love—metamorphosis attains its full reality. A relationship which for us seemed to hold the meaning of existence—and, as such, established the coordinates of our life—vanishes into infinity. Time devours even our experience of a possible passionate attachment to another human

---

[79] *Remembrance of Things Past,* 1:1089.
[80] *Remembrance of Things Past,* 1:1089.
[81] *Remembrance of Things Past,* 1:691.

being, "as we so painfully discover when we are in love and would like to believe in the unique reality of the beloved."[82] The admiration we feel for another, elicited by our passion, dominates— according to Proust—our need: "to give our happiness its full meaning, we would rather preserve for all those separate points of our desire, at the very moment in which we succeed in touching them ... the distinction of being intangible."[83] We have lived for decades with the loved one death has taken from us, and we begin to feel that what we considered to be a sacred intimacy might be replaced by new relationships. Must we then free ourselves of our past? Must we live the passion of new hopes and new sorrows? This would mean burying, denying all that we have been: "... he feared death itself no more than such a recovery, which would in fact amount to the death of all that he now was."[84]

What then is the meaning of our struggle? Do we struggle simply to repeat a performance, a story, a scene? Passions lead us to new encounters, to new characters, one after the other. Do we fall prey to illusion when we speak of them as 'sacred'? Could it be that only passion is sacred? "I said to myself that this love of ours, in so far as it is a love for one particular creature, is not perhaps a very real thing."[85] Well then, we can legitimately say with Proust that all these questions constitute "those mysteries whose explanation is to be found probably only in worlds other than our own and the presentiment of which is the thing that moves us most deeply in life and in art."[86]

Can it be that the only valid thing left is the appeal of the abyss, wherein we exist as characters playing our assigned parts in a quick succession of scenes and acts? Will we ever overcome the cruelty of the appeal of existence, which reveals itself as indifference for the individual, as the relentless demand on the individual to play an ever-changing succession of roles? And as a result, will we never cease to wonder whether passions pertain to human beings at all, or whether they are solely the expressions of the magical essence of life?

---

[82] *Remembrance of Things Past,* 1:576.
[83] *Remembrance of Things Past,* 1:578.
[84] *Remembrance of Things Past,* 1:327.
[85] *Remembrance of Things Past,* 1:691.
[86] *Remembrance of Things Past,* 3:1089.

# The Word Speaks for Itself: Novalis

## 1) The Ideal of Aprioristic Philosophy

In order to interpret Proust's language and his theories we must keep in mind the system of aprioristic philosophy which, in striking contrast to what we have been trying to illustrate so far, denies philosophical validity to thought based on sensory and artistic experience. Traditional philosophy claims to be able to identify objectivity through rationality and, consequently, attempts to exclude from its realm all that can distract from the rational determination of individual beings, namely, every thought and every word connected to sensibility, time, place, passions.

The definition of man as *zoon logon echon* revolves around the interpretation of *logos* as reason rather than language, and thus becomes determining for the Western philosophical tradition. To deny *ratio* its supremacy would entail a relapse into irrationality. All that presupposes as well the denial of the philosophical function of metaphor, since the transference (*metapherein*) of the meaning of a term rationally defined invalidates the principle of *verbum proprium*, the product of rational process.

The transpositions, the metaphors, the images which replace the concept threaten the logical process and cloud its clarity.

German Idealism defines philosophy as the science of rational, systematic thought which grasps the essence of reality solely through a dialectical process. Hegel states that in order to reach "the different stages of the determination of the Idea in its logical concept," it is necessary that "the fundamental concepts of the systems that have appeared in the history of philosophy ... be separated from what concerns their external formation, their application to particulars, and similar things."[1] Philosophy attains its proper form only when it rises to the level of the absolute *Idea*, without indulging in imagination or art, which use inadequate forms of expression. From this position Hegel theorized the death of art in the age when philosophy had clearly and consciously acknowledged the supremacy of ideas.

That also explains how, both in Idealism and Kant's criticism, metaphoric thought and language are identified with rhetoric, which is accorded only the function of persuasion. "The linguistic arts are eloquence and poetry. Eloquence is the art of treating an intellectual task as if it were a free play of the imagination ... the orator promises something serious and carries it out as if it were a simple play of ideas for the entertainment of the spectators."[2] Kant's goal is to safeguard the pre-eminence of reason, since the rational becomes universal and necessary only if we base it exclusively on *a priori* forms of knowledge. For this reason, any form of thought which does not conform to this fundamental principle is judged to be the expression of a trivial 'common sense,' and, as such, is rejected. "When knowledge of universals is obtained from the particular, we have common sense (*der gemeine Verstand, sensus communis*) ... only when knowledge of particulars is derived from individuals, we have science (*concretum ab abstracto*)."[3] "To appeal to common sense when knowledge and intelligence are insufficient, and not before, is one of the subtleties found in our times... But as long as we can still think a little, we shall guard ourselves against recourse to this extreme solution."[4]

Accordingly, Fichte states that transcendental thought cannot be deduced from experience, and that therefore life and philosophy are two radically different things. "To live is properly not to philosophize; to philosophize is properly not to live... We are here before a radical antithesis, and it is impossible to find a point of concurrence."[5]

---

[1] G. W. F. Hegel, *Vorlesungen uber die Geschichte der Philosophie*, in *Samtliche Werke* (Stuttgart: Frommann, 1928), 17:59.

[2] I. Kant, *Kritik des Urteilskraft*, in *Gesammelte Schriften* (Berlin: Gruyter, 1913), 5:321.

[3] I. Kant, *Kant's handschriftlicher Nachlass*, Band III, *Logik* (Berlin: Gruyter, 1924), 16:18 n. 1579.

[4] I. Kant, *Prolegomena zu einer jeden künftigen Metaphysik die als Wissenschaft wird auftreten können* (Berlin: Gruyter, 1911), 4:259.

[5] J. G. Fichte, *Rückeinnerungen, Antworten, Fragen*, in *Nachgelassene Schriften*

The Western philosophical tradition maintains that the quests which must shape our lives are the quests for truth and rational knowledge. Science—and philosophy claims to be a science—is identified with the rational process, whose consequences are predetermined by its initial premise: the pattern we must follow is mathematical and geometrical. It follows that the only goal pursued by the rational process is to demonstrate and to explain; therefore, when it is confronted with sensible phenomena, it defines and clarifies them on the basis of their own foundation, of their primary axiom.

As a result, knowledge is elaborated on progressively more anonymous terms, since rational principles, adhering as they must to necessity and universality, are not bound to individual beings. Personal and biographical data which may emerge in the course of a scientific investigation are excluded from philosophical analysis and are said to belong to the prehistory of the psyche: "The I that constitutes the point of departure of science ... is ... the identity of he who has consciousness and of the thing that he has consciousness of, and we can arrive at this distinction only by means of an abstraction from all that pertains to the personality."[6] In this context, stylistic problems are nonsensical, unacceptable to philosophy, which values only rational abstract language. Style is taken into consideration only in so far as it communicates scientific material to a large public in a comprehensible manner. In this case, however, style is debased to the level of mere vulgarization.

And so after Kant, Hegel states that philosophy is intrinsically *esoteric*, and therefore "not made for the populace, nor is it capable of educating it [*Weder für den Pöbel gemacht, noch einer Zubereitung für den Pöble fähig*]."[7]

True thoughts and scientific insight are only to be won through the labour of the Notion. Only the Notion can produce the universality of knowledge which is neither common

---

*1796–1801, Gesamtausgabe*, ed. R. Lauth and H. Gliwitzky (Stuttgart: Frommann, 1979), II, 5, p. 119.

[6] J. G. Fichte, *Sonnenklarer Bericht an der grössere Publikum über das eigentliche Wesen der neuesten Philosophie (1801), Gesamtausgabe*, I, 7, p. 235.

[7] G. W. F. Hegel, *Über das Wesen der philosophischen Kritik überhaupt, und ihr Verhältniss zum gegenwärtigen Zustand der Philosophie insbesondere*, in *Sämtliche Werke*, 1:185.

vagueness nor the inadequacy of ordinary common sense, but a fully developed, perfected cognition; not the uncommon universality of a reason whose talents have been ruined by indolence and the conceit of genius, but a truth ripened to its properly matured form so as to be capable of being the property of all self-conscious Reason.[8]

According to Fichte, the point of departure of philosophy and science can be deduced only from an act of consciousness, understood as a fundamentally self-realizing process. His concept of system is rooted in two basic principles: that of action (*Tat*), and that of consciousness (*Beuresstseinsakt*), this time understood as the source of scientific knowledge.

A series of propositions—writes Fichte—constitutes a scientific structure only if they are grouped together in a context; therefore, the first essential structure of any science must be a systematic structure. Since philosophy is the quest for first principles, each individual science must conform to these principles.

Fichte's reasoning proceeds as follows: If our knowledge were not a single system "our house would then be truly well-built, but not as a single well-connected building, but as an aggregate of rooms, from none of which we could enter the other; it would be a house in which we would forever lose ourselves and where we would never be at home."[9]

Fichte's thesis is based on the principle that scientific fundamentals must simultaneously have *form* and *content* and no need of proof.[10] Fichte's point of departure is the identity principle (A is A), since no one can deny it without necessarily presupposing it first; in that sense, it is a *fundamental, basic principle* (*Grundsatz*). It is, however, a purely formal principle since it presupposes that A exists. In fact, Fichte notes, it affirms that only if A *is*, then A *is* A. The relation between the 'only if' and the 'then' is one of necessity. We must, therefore, ask ourselves where and how such a relation is established.

---

[8] G. W. F. Hegel, *Phenomenology of Spirit*, tr. A.V. Miller (Oxford: Clarendon Press, 1977), 43.

[9] J.G. Fichte, *Über den Begriff der Wissenschaftslehre, Werke 1793–1795*, in *Gesamtausgabe*, I, 2, p. 125.

[10] Fichte, I, 2, p. 117.

Fichte maintained that it is established in the Ego, through an act of self-consciousness, by virtue of the identity principle ('I' = 'I'), since it is only here that we can find identity of form and content. Consequently, only what is deduced from consciousness can claim to be real. Such thesis corresponds to the power accorded to the principle: "We must search for the principle of all human knowledge, the principle which is absolutely the first and absolutely unconditional. Since it must be the absolute first principle, it cannot be determined and it cannot be demonstrated. It must initiate that act which does not figure, and which could not figure, among the empirical demonstrations of our consciousness, but which lies rather at the base of every consciousness, and only makes it possible."[11] Thus, Fichte's arguments culminate in the apotheosis of a self-determining science which deduces all reality from consciousness. "Philosophy teaches us to search for everything in the I. Only through the I, order and harmony reach the dead and formless populace."[12]

It is important to note that, in German Idealism, the ego's activity (Fichte's *Tätigkeit*) is not only accorded absolute pre-eminence, it also necessarily implies deducing reality a priori, logically, in a completely abstract and rigorously systematic manner. The *Tathandlung*, for Fichte the originary act of the spirit, is realized in Hegel through a dialectical scheme.

Hegel, in his evaluation of Kant in the introduction to his *Phenomenology of Spirit*, notes that critical philosophy begins with the thesis that the problem of determining the forms of knowledge precedes any philosophical investigation; it thus comes to declare the pre-eminence of epistemology, as Kant maintained in *Prolegomena to any Future Metaphysics*.

Hegel rejects the notion that a theory of knowledge can be a propaedeutic to philosophy. He states that we must reject "such useless ideas and locutions about cognition as 'an instrument for getting hold of the Absolute' or as a medium through which we view the truth."[13] Such a position presupposes

---

[11] Fichte, *Grundlage der gesammten Wissenschaftslehre als Handschrift für seine Zuhörer*, in *Gesamtausgabe*, I, 2, p. 255.

[12] *Uber die Würde des menschen*, in *Gesamtausgabe*, I, 2, p. 87.

[13] *Phenomenology of Spirit*, 48.

ideas about cognition as an *instrument* and as a *medium*, and assumes that there is a *difference between ourselves and this cognition*. Above all, it presupposes that the Absolute stands on one side and cognition on the other, independent and separated from it, and yet is something real; or in other words, it presupposes that cognition which, since it is excluded from the Absolute, is surely outside of the truth as well, is nevertheless true.[14]

Dialectic thus offers us, in its every act of synthesis, a figure that identifies the rational with the real. The succession of theses which consciousness progressively acknowledges results in the education (*Bildung*) of *consciousness* to the level of *science*: "The series of configurations which consciousness goes through along this road is, in reality, the detailed history of the *education* of consciousness itself to the standpoint of science."[15]

Hence, Hegel's conclusive thesis, which is twofold: All that is real is rational, and therefore all that is real must be deduced *a priori*. Moreover, every pathetic, subjective, and perceptible element must be considered exclusively in its rational aspect.

In his *Encyclopaedia*, Hegel stated that philosophy is a rational speculation which replaces representations with concepts and categories, and which has the ultimate aim of apprehending reality through the dialectical method, solely on the basis of logic, by excluding from it any and all objects of experience. For this reason, art and poetry precede philosophy because they reveal the Idea only in its perceptible form, as the *Ideal* which does not correspond to superior forms of thought.[16] Art, therefore, loses its legitimacy in the age of absolute reason. The real task of art "is to bring to consciousness the supreme interests of the spirit"; art is not "the supreme form of the spirit" and the work of art is not "thought and concept, but the development of the concept from itself and alienation in the sensible."[17]

---

[14] *Phenomenology of Spirit*, 47.

[15] *Phenomenology of Spirit*, 50.

[16] G.W.F. Hegel, *Vorlesungen uber die Aesthetik*, in *Sämtliche Werke* (Stuttgart: 1928), 12:32.

[17] Hegel, 12:34.

In fact, the concept is the universal which remains within its own particularization, which goes beyond itself and its own other, and which is therefore the power and the action which transcend the alienation towards which it moves. The same is true of art in which thought alienates itself: It belongs to the sphere of conceptual thought, and the spirit, by subjecting it to scientific considerations, satisfies nothing other than the need of its own most intimate nature.[18]

## 2) *The Philosophical Significance of German Romanticism:* Novalis's Monolog

Our analysis of Proust has brought us to the conclusion that he, too, ultimately rejects the duality of knowing subject and object since he, in fact, acknowledges each individual being as the expression of a more profound reality which manifests itself in our experience of language. The originary function of language cannot be denied, but that very fact causes us to face an additional problem. If language is not a function of beings, then what does it speak for, what originary reality does it disclose?

In German Romanticism we find that the originary manifestation of reality is not identified with the rational dialectical process, but rather with the existential experience of language. The originary act, which Fichte termed *Tathandlung*, becomes here the underivable, groundless experience of the word.

At this point, two problems arise: one theoretical, one historical. Let us look at the theoretical problem first. It would seem that any discussion on being, and any conclusion we might reach on the subject, are based on individual beings. Individual beings, in fact, participate in and are 'participles' of being, and the ontological difference attests to the fact that they are, therefore, indissolubly linked with each other. But can language, while it refers to individual beings, also speak of being? What is the aim of language? Is not the determination of individual beings its originary task?

Now for the historical problem: Idealism, in its most historically accomplished form, which is Hegelian philosophy, considered

---

[18] Hegel, 12:34–35.

Romanticism marginal to philosophical thought, and regarded it primarily as a 'literary' phenomenon. But does not its neglected philosophical significance lie in the fact that language, in contrast to the perspective of traditional philosophy, is not the expressive agent of individual beings? Does not its philosophical specificity lie in the fact that it starts, not with the problem of individual beings, but with that of the word? But of what does the word, of what does language speak if not of individual beings? We can resume discussing our thesis on the originary nature and underivedness of the sounds of language with the help of an eminent representative of German Romanticism: Novalis. I shall refer to his work entitled *Monolog*, written in 1798. Our analysis of it will give us the opportunity, not only to reassess the philosophical contribution made by Romanticism, but also to test the validity of the traditional scheme of ontological metaphysics, which designates individual beings as its point of departure.

The text reads:

> Strange things are said about speaking and writing. Even genuine conversations are but a game of words. The ridiculous mistake, which we ought to marvel at, is that people think they speak of things. But no one knows the peculiarity of language, that it is concerned only with itself. This is the reason why language is such a wonderful and fruitful mystery. If someone speaks only for the sake of speaking, it is then that he really expresses the greatest, most original truths.[19]

These opening sentences by Novalis formulate a threefold thesis: Language is a game; language does not speak (as is generally thought) in order to bring about the determination of individual beings; language occurs only as a function of itself.

First of all, let us ask ourselves: What could the statement that language occurs only as a function of itself and not of individual beings ('Language is concerned only with itself') mean? Such a statement seems tautological and nonsensical. But why? The starting point of traditional philosophy is individual beings, beings it wants to define rationally. The problem it considers originary, then, is that of

[19] Novalis, *Schriften*, Zweiter band: *Das philosophische Werk I, Studien zur bildenden Kunst*, ed. R. Samuel, H. J. Mahl, G. Schulz (Stuttgart: Kohlhammer, 1981), 672.

beings, not language. It deals with language only in so far as it expresses the rational determinations of beings. But if language no longer has such a role, what is then its task? In order to answer this question, we must examine the concept of 'game,' which is central in Novalis, who in fact states that language, that dialogue, is a *game of words*.

## 3) The Structure of the Game

*First*: Every game uses elements, instruments which are real, such as cards, dice, a football, colors, sounds. We define these elements, the individual beings, as instruments of the game because they are means to the achievement of its goal. In other words, if we adopted Greek terminology, we could say that these instruments have a *poietic* function in the sense that they are not an end in themselves, that they serve a purpose. They become, therefore, superfluous when they have served this purpose and the aim has been achieved. It doesn't make sense to continue to build once we have completed what we had intended to build. Furthermore, we must note that the games cited above, football, dice and card games, constitute only diversion, 'entertainment,' and are devoid of any existential meaning. The rules by which they are played are arbitrarily set.

*Second*: In order to be played, besides instruments (concrete beings such as playing cards, dice, footballs), every game needs rules. The instruments—that is the beings used in the game—become the very vehicle of playfulness when and if they are used in the context of those rules.

It is also crucial to point out that the rules, which the instruments obey and which distinguish one game from another, are not deducible from the instruments of the game, as evidenced by the fact that these same playing cards and dice and footballs can be used in very different games. The code of each individual game, the one single thing which can reveal the instruments' purposefulness, cannot be inferred from the instrumental beings themselves. On the contrary, the purposefulness of an instrument can be understood only by knowing the rules of the game, by knowing the code. For this reason, the rules of the game must be clearly set out before the game starts, they must be invented by a subject, an individual. It is evident, then, that the code is arbitrary—and it is apparently so for every game—and that it has an *individual* quality to it. Games can become diversions only because they originate from an individual.

*Third*: Games do not only involve instruments and rules, but also facts and actions which are different for every game. The action involved in a card game is different from the actions we perform when we play dice or football. A game is meaningless if we fail to perform the action which is peculiar to that game.

What does the game reveal as it is played? What does the action required by the game disclose? Certainly not the abstract rules of the game, since these are mere presuppositions; and not even the players' knowledge of the instruments. In performing the required actions, nobody plays, for example, for the cards or the dice themselves, but for the possibilities hidden in the game, possibilities which are impossible to identify *a priori*, before the game starts. Hence, the spectators' curiosity. The possibilities unfold as the story of each match unfolds. Furthermore, each match has its own history as well. And recalling the record of what has already taken place entails two metaphysical activities, since dice are not only small wooden cubes and playing cards mere color-printed cardboard pieces, nor are single matches similar to each other, for each action taken in each match always carries with it new meanings. Games, moreover, at the moment they are being played, reveal the players' passions and traits, their anguish in the face of defeat, their hope to win.

What the actions of a game reveal is an entire world, a cosmos, an order, which unfolds in its historicity before our very eyes, before us, the spectators. Clearly, the activities of playing and observing the play do not necessarily express a theory of knowledge, nor a rational determination of individual beings, nor a difference between *phenomenon* and *noumenon*, nor an abstract metaphysics. Hence, the spectators' curiosity. The spectators are attracted and fascinated by what is new in every game, in every match, in the history of the game.

## 4) Novalis and Idealism

If we wanted to track down the roots of Novalis's theories, to go back to his first critical encounter with Idealism and trace the development of his thought, we would have to start with the fragments of 1795–1797. That is exactly what Theodor Haering tried to do in his *Novalis als Philosoph*.[20] However, whether Haering's concept of

---

[20] T. Haering, *Novalis als Philosoph* (Stuttgart: Kohlhammer, 1954).

philosophy, which he presupposed in order to assess Novalis's thought, truly constitutes the most profitable way to read the author remains to be seen.

Novalis had already become interested in Kant and Idealism at Jena and Leipzig (1792–1793). In 1795, he met Fichte and was close to Holderlin. It is thought that he had been studying Fichte as early as 1794. In a letter to Friedrich Schlegel dated July 8, 1796, he acknowledged his indebtedness to Fichte for his encouragement, since it was he who had awakened him and enriched his spiritual life.[21] It is certain that his interest in Fichte was very strong as early as the fall of 1795.

However, in another letter, also to Schlegel, dated June 14, 1797, he stated: "I am indebted to you and to your thought-provoking free critical spirit for the many indications and instructions that have guided me through his [Fichte's] terrible intertwinement of abstractions."[22]

Perhaps it is possible to see already the attitude which he would later fully display toward Idealism in the following observations on Kant: "Kant's entire method, his entire philosophy is unilateral and could be rightfully termed scholastic. It is certainly the greatest of its kind, one of the most remarkable phenomena of the human spirit."[23] Another fragment, one we shall have to bear in mind in the course of our considerations, seems to be a programmatic challenge to traditional metaphysics: "To destroy the principle of contradiction; this is perhaps the supreme task of superior logic."[24]

Novalis's disillusionment with Idealism had already begun in 1797, when he took up studying the Dutch philosopher Franz Hemsterhuys (1721–1790). Novalis knew his works well; in fact, in a letter to his brother August Wilhelm, dated January 1792 at Leipzig, Schlegel wrote that "his [Novalis's] favourite authors are Plato and Hemsterhuys."[25] Up to 1792, Hemsterhuys's works in French had only been published separately in very limited numbers of copies. In 1787, Herder had published a translation of the *Lettre sur le désir* in "Teutschen Merkur."

---

[21] Novalis, *Schriften*, 4:188.
[22] Novalis, *Schriften*, 4:230.
[23] Novalis, *Schriften*, 2:392, n. 50.
[24] Novalis, *Schriften*, 3:570, n. 101.
[25] Letter quoted in 2:310.

It seems that for Novalis the issue of individual beings, and consequently the issue of a theory of knowledge, is no longer on the foreground; he is concerned, instead, with man's coming to presence. In a fragment he writes:

> The most wonderful phenomenon, the eternal phenomenon is our own existence. Man's greatest mystery is man himself. The resolution of the endless action of this task is to be found in universal history. The history of philosophy as the noblest of all sciences, of literature as substance, records attempts at ideal solutions to this ideal problem—to this idea thought out by the mind.[26]

But what did Novalis mean by the affirmation that man's greatest mystery is his own existence? Did he mean it in an idealistic sense? Did he interpret it in the sense of a Kantian theory of knowledge of individual beings? How did he see the solution to this task actually taking shape as the history of the world? In a Fichtean sense?

## 5) *The Fundamental Importance of Novalis's Theory of the Game of Language*

Let us now take a closer look at the threefold thesis formulated by Novalis in his *Monolog*. It does not concern just any game, but a particular kind: the game of words. Novalis's statements are in striking opposition to the Western philosophical tradition, whose point of departure is individual beings; ontology, not language. In the belief that the language of logic is the only objective language, this tradition gives it predominance above all others. Lastly, the Western philosophical tradition acknowledges in language the function of disclosing the meaning of beings.

Novalis's threefold thesis drastically transforms such conceptions. He states not only that language is a game, but that it is a game which occurs independently of things, which is "concerned only with itself." We become fully aware of the significance of this thesis as we read the other statements made by Novalis in the *Monolog*. After noting that mathematical formulas as well "constitute a world of their own, play exclusively among themselves" and that they become

---

[26] Novalis, *Schriften*, 2:362.

'members of nature' only by virtue of human freedom, he solemnly and polemically declares:

> The same goes for language. He who has a fine sense of its touch, rhythm, and musical soul, he who senses in himself the subtle action of its intimate nature and moves his tongue or his pen accordingly, he will be a prophet. By contrast, he who knows all this but lacks a sufficiently good ear and a sufficiently good grasp of it, he will be mocked by language and laughed at by men, as the Trojans laughed at Cassandra.[27]

Novalis was well aware that his thesis was tremendously innovative and therefore difficult to comprehend, for he added the following remark: "While I believe that with this I have explained in the clearest possible manner the essence and the role of poetry, I also know that there is no one who can understand it."[28]

Even before we attempt any critical interpretation of the text, we notice that Novalis, unexpectedly, relates the problem of language to that of poetry, that is to metaphorical image-creating language. The game, in the general sense of the term, and the game of language have in common the requirement of sense perceptions, since no game at all is possible otherwise. Language, however, does not play with dice or cards, but with sounds, which are nevertheless real.

We must, then, first of all discuss the radical difference between games in general and games of language. But is not this difference self-evident in so far as games are escapist and amusing while games of language are not? Let us answer this question by further examining the structure of games of words.

The second factor determining the structure of the game as such is the fact that it needs playing rules. These constitute the code of the game since, through their agency, the instruments acquire meaning, and games distinguish themselves from each other.

The fundamental difference between the two types of game lies in the fact that in games in general the code is arbitrarily chosen, a characteristic which determines their entertainment function. The play of language, instead, intends to manifest the disclosure of beings,

---

[27] Novalis, *Schriften*, 2:672.
[28] Ibid.

of the being of beings; accordingly, being as such constitutes the rule of the game, the code for the game of language, since individual beings participate in and are 'participles' of being as such. The code for this type of game, then, cannot be arbitrary or subjective, since it does not concern the isolated instance of a being, but the being of beings. The game of language is objective in the extreme. It does not constitute diversion, escapism or relaxation. On the contrary, it is extremely intense and requires our full concentration; it is the originary effort and the burden of our existence, of our being-there. Since the game of language is the urgent manifestation of a given being, being as such is its code, the means which discloses the individual being in its being or its meaning. In the matches of history, we play for and lose not only the possibilities of our individuality and our world, but also our performances as winners or losers.

The third factor determining the essence of games in general, their fundamental characteristic, is that they have to be played, for only the events, the actions performed as required by the game, can reveal what the code conceals as *possibilities*. In this respect, the two types of game are similar, except for the nature of the possibilities. The game of language entails the possibilities available to being, the possibilities of its coming to presence and of its history, and it is the occurrence of the newness which grips our curiosity.

However, if at this point the two types of game display a certain resemblance, it is also at this stage that they prove to be radically different. Language makes real the announcement, which is forever new, of a world, of an order, of a cosmos, and of our corresponding historical world. Every individual being emerges in the game of language in all its compelling historical meaning. The code, being as such, appears as the game is being played, on the basis of the first *originary indications*—which therefore are not proofs—as they occur in our experience which finds an originary expression in our cry, in the joy and despair that move us. Pain or suffering has primacy because it is with it that we experience a world that is on the wane for us, a world which can, however, point to a new world which, in turn, can announce its coming only through the presence of a dominant order. All of that constitutes the seriousness of the game of language, since it is in and through language that we make it known, that we express it; it is the *explicatio* of an originary *implicatio*. In its essence, language is not a diversion.

As the expression of our response to the appeal of being, language discloses our history as individuals, as players, in diverse situations, bearing the suffering that they comport, situations in which the code mercilessly imposes itself on us. Every individual being, therefore, is identical and, at the same time, not identical with itself, since it comes to presence in and through the code, which is not arbitrarily invented, but passionately experienced. Every individual being, then, must be interpreted only on the basis of the code. And that—as we have already hinted—is the origin of the metaphorical nature of every originary language.

## 6) Romanticizing the World: The System

Let me now refer to fragment 105 of Novalis's preliminary work of 1798:

> The world must be romanticized. Then we will rediscover its primordial sense. Romanticization is nothing but a strengthening of qualities. In the course of this action, the inferior I is identified with the superior I. We are ourselves a qualitative series of powers. This operation is still completely unknown. In so far as I confer a higher sense to the ordinary, an enigmatic character to the usual, the dignity of the unknown to the known, the semblance of infinity to the finite, I romanticize it…and it receives a current expression. Romantic philosophy. *Lingua romana.*[29]

Romanticizing, as Novalis states, is not a theory, a task accomplished by logic, but an action, a *praxis*. As a result, Novalis distinguishes two completely different levels of reality: the level of the ordinary, the usual, the known, the finite, and that of the higher sense, the enigmatic character, the dignity of the unknown, the semblance of infinity.

The level of the ordinary belongs to those who acknowledge only individual beings and want to adhere to them exclusively, unable to grasp their radical transience. Instead, "life is the beginning of death. Life exists because of death. Death is both an end and a beginning, a separation from and, at the same time, a more intimate union with,

---

[29] Novalis, *Schriften,* 2:545, n. 105.

oneself."[30] Novalis further declares:

> The Philistines live only everyday lives. The primary means seems to be their only end. Apparently, as they themselves admit and as is indeed the case, they do all that for the love of earthly life. They infuse very little poetry into it, and this they do only because they are now used to certain interruptions in their daily life.[31]

The sphere of the ordinary, the usual, in which all coincides perfectly, without any differentiation, is the sphere where men desperately cling to individual beings, believing in and asserting only their stable identities. This same sphere must be made to undergo a transformation which Novalis defines through opposites: The known must be juxtaposed with "the dignity of the unknown";[32] all that the majority of men no longer see in everyday life must be made visible; all that is concealed in individual beings must be awakened and made noticeable; the finite must be contrasted with the semblance of infinity. The action Novalis advocates is not, then, a rejection of the ordinary in a Platonic sense, whereby what is valid must be transposed to an ahistorical world; it is, instead, a new evaluation and a deeper understanding of everyday life: "Then we will rediscover its primordial sense."[33]

We must subject beings to new appraisals; more specifically, we must look for their higher sense. Novalis states that this action "is completely unknown," and adds: "We search everywhere for the absolute, and we are forever finding mere things."[34] This transformation, which Novalis describes by juxtapositions, relates to our 'higher I'; it is, then, something that concerns us all, solemn and significant, not accidental, as may instead occur in a purely literary or aesthetic operation. It concerns our very own being. Nor is it a subjective, arbitrary transformation capable of creating reality. This operation, instead, discloses, in Novalis's words, the primordial sense

---

[30] Novalis, *Schriften*, 2:416, n. 15.
[31] Novalis, *Schriften*, 2:446, n. 76.
[32] Novalis, *Schriften*, 2:545, n. 105.
[33] Ibid.
[34] Novalis, *Schriften*, 2:412, n. 1.

of reality; it causes us to discover it and to subordinate ourselves to it. The operation Novalis speaks of reveals new possibilities of unconcealment for individual beings, possibilities which could not become manifest if we adhered to their abstract or rational definitions. In such a purview, poetry, which is to say metaphorical-poetic language, is not an interruption in a unilateral reflection on existing things.

It is, therefore, a matter of finding the 'sense' of 'the ordinary,' of that in which everything comes together without differentiations; individual beings thus attain a 'higher sense,' an 'enigmatic character'. What that means is surrendering to the game of language. The ordinary then suddenly becomes unsettling. "Thought is but a dream of perceptiveness, an exhausted perceptiveness, a feeble, gray, pale life."[35] Now we must 'romanticize' the world and cause its premises to unfold; in other words, we must play the involving game of language, wagering ourselves and our world in it. Precisely because being cannot be apprehended through a rational definition of individual beings, it discloses itself in the historicity of the game of language, in our responses to its appeals which are different in every situation and in which being reveals itself in ever different forms, manifesting sameness and difference at the same time.

On the matter of the appeal of being, Novalis asks:

> Could it be that the supreme principle includes within it the supreme paradox? That it is a thesis which simply does not appease but forever attracts and repels, forever becoming incomprehensible every time we have understood it? A thesis which stimulates us into activity without ever tiring us, without this action ever becoming a habit?

And then he adds: "According to ancient mystical legends, God is something similar to this for the spirits."[36]

But then is language something similar to the divine for Novalis? The word, as the disclosure of individual beings in relation to the call of being, has a metaphorical role: It points to something on the ground of this appeal, which is always different. Order, the world, manifests itself in the history of metaphorical language where every

---

[35] Novalis, *Schriften*, 1:96.
[36] Novalis, *Schriften*, 2:523–524, n. 9.

word is identical with itself and with another: "Man: a metaphor."[37]

But is there a being which is not found within language—understood as a response to the appeal—and which is therefore not equivalent to an instrument employed for the realization of our being-there?

Does Novalis formulate the problem of the relation between the 'corporeal' and the 'spiritual'? If so, how does he solve it? In order to answer these questions we must refer to a long fragment, number 111, which is also part of his preliminary work of 1798.

> We have two sense systems which, however different they might appear, are nevertheless intimately connected. One system is called the body, the other the soul. The former is dependent upon external stimuli, the combination of which we call nature or the external world. The latter originally depends on a series of internal stimuli, which we call spirit or the spiritual world. Usually, this last system is linked with the other by an associative relation and is influenced by it. However, we frequently notice evidence of the opposite relation, and soon we note that the two systems should actually exist in a perfectly reciprocal correspondence whereby each, influenced by its own world, would sound with the other in perfect unison, rather than in a monotone. In short, the two worlds, and the two systems, ought to form neither a disharmony, nor a monotony, but a free harmony. Undoubtedly, the passage from monotony to harmony will occur through disharmony—and only at the end harmony will emerge. In periods of belief in magic, the body is believed to serve the soul or the spiritual world. (Madness-Exaltation).[38]

"Ordinary madness ceases to be madness and becomes magic, a self-conscious madness abiding by rules."[39]

'System' here generally indicates the arrangement of multiple elements on the basis of principles which constitute the foundation of that system and which therefore play a hermeneutic and dominant

---

[37] Novalis, *Schriften,* 2:561, n. 174.
[38] Novalis, *Schriften,* 2:546–547, n. 111.
[39] Novalis, *Schriften,* 2:546–547, n. 111.

role (*arché*) in relation to the multiplicity surrounding them. Those ordering principles actually constitute the code of the system. In a 1796 note appended to his studies on Fichte, Novalis remarks:

> Every explanation must begin with a fact (*Thatsache*). But what is this fact from which every explanation must derive? There must necessarily be a fact upon which all the others are based, which itself needs no explanation, which alone makes every explanation possible. Explanations then emerge from the fact of every fact or from the one single original fact. It must be inexplicable, that is to say, its most complete concept must be innate in it... It is explicable because it exists, and it exists because it has been explained.[40]

We shall not dwell now on what Fichte meant by the term 'fact,' but on what Novalis means by it. For Novalis, the principle determining the 'fact' as *arché* establishes itself and asserts itself of necessity. But what does 'fact' mean in his system? It is certainly not an object (*objectum*) of a theory. Such an interpretation of the term would clash with what we have read in Novalis so far. It would also contrast with the following statement: "The world is set against its cause. The cause is the quality of the world and the world is the quality of the cause." Soon after this statement, Novalis adds a reference to God: "God is simultaneously both the cause and the world."[41] Are we confronted here with a traditional idea? But if the world comes to being through the game of language and manifests itself in its coming, then the origin of coming to being must lie in the facticity of the word and not in any other object. God can be identified only with this occurrence, only with history in its unfolding. This is how the divine is determined.

If the world is a cosmos, an order and an ornament, then it emerges from the game of language and, for this reason, the occurrence of language is groundless and inexplicable. We have groundlessness in the principles or in the foundations. Novalis asks: "But why do we have these and not some others? This is a problem which is

---

[40] Novalis, *Schriften*, 2:265, n. 554.
[41] Novalis, *Schriften*, 2:236, n. 425.

not a problem ... since it is so, really so."[42]

From Novalis's considerations in fragment 111, around which our discussion revolves, it is clear that the system, the world, is neither created by man, by a subject aiming at a code, nor is it explained by a theory of knowledge; the world is, rather, passionately experienced by the body and the soul:

> One system is called the body, the other the soul ... the latter originally depends on a series of internal stimuli which we call spirit.... Usually, this last system is linked with the other by means of an associative relation.... However, we frequently notice evidence of the opposite relation....[43]

The origin of that which appears is the impulse of being toward its manifestation in a cosmos, in an order. This impulse acts and then, in Meister Eckhart's words, torments the individual being, which bears testimony to the appeal. The being of beings is not deducible from individual beings, which are only the manifestation of being as such, which is disclosed to man in and through the game of language.

And so, in striking contrast to traditional thought, we have Novalis's thesis, now with disturbing resonance: Passions do not originate from objects; passions, instead, are themselves the origin of the meaning of beings. In fragment 101, he explicitly states that passions are a function of the act of seeing, that particular act of seeing in which the world discloses itself: "The eye is the vocal organ of feelings. Visible objects are expressions of feelings."[44]

We must search for that which has no foundation precisely because that is what constantly appears in our painful enduring, in our knowledge, and in our experience of the transience of beings, of every objective datum. "All which is visible is attached to the invisible, the audible to the inaudible, the sensible to the insensible. Perhaps, the thinkable to the unthinkable."[45] Our task, therefore, is to romanticize the world. However, it is not possible to 'romanticize' on the basis of a rational theory, a theory of knowledge, which

---

[42] Novalis, *Schriften*, 2:246, n. 452.
[43] Novalis, *Schriften*, 2:546–547, n. 111.
[44] Novalis, *Schriften*, 2:545, n. 101.
[45] Novalis, *Schriften*, 2:650, n. 481.

claims to represent the presupposition of all future philosophies. We must attain romanticization in the anguish we feel in the face of chaos.

Novalis's thesis—that there are two systems, a corporeal one and a spiritual one, and that the relation they share establishes neither a monotony, nor a disharmony, but a harmony—carries within it the rigorous concept of Romanticism, free from any subjectivism and from any sentimental psychology. In another fragment, Novalis states: "Elements of Romanticism. Objects, like the notes of an aeolian harp, must emerge all at once, without a cause—without revealing their instrument."[46]

Let us now return to a consideration made in connection with Proust. We cannot play an instrument and arrive at musical facticity if the instrument, the means to achieve this end, is not tuned. In our conception of music, we generally emphasize the contribution of the composer or that of the virtuoso interpreting the score, and in so doing we conceive music or harmony primarily as a man's creation; we forget that at the bottom of it all there is the originary tuning of the instrument. It alone makes the possibilities of music audible, and the individual being which is the instrument is merely a witness to the fact. The essence of Novalis's concept of romanticism raises the notes, the instruments, the actions, to this higher level. The intonation on the basis of which we tune our musical instruments in order to raise our musical games to the level of actuality is to be explained neither with tones nor with recorded notes, which are individual beings, but with the spiritual world of harmony in which we live.

Let us recall once again Novalis's words: "Usually, this last system [of the spirit] is linked with the other [of the body] by means of an associative relation. . . . However, we frequently notice evidence of the opposite relation."[47] It is important to note that here, as in the fragment on the romanticization of the world, we find the term 'usually,' which is equivalent to that notion of 'the ordinary' whose sense the process of romanticization makes more profound.

We were born into a continuous death, and what reveals itself to us is strange, since we believe, as when we are in a concert hall, that the notes, or the game of the particular, constitute the originary, and

---

[46] Novalis, *Schriften*, 3:558, n. 17.
[47] Novalis, *Schriften*, 2:546, n. 111.

we forget the 'system' evoking them in their musical significance. Therefore, harmony, the system, consists of the disharmony between being and concrete beings: The world of individual beings is not the world of being as such. Harmony without disharmony gives rise to uniformity, monotony; besides, there is no harmony without disharmony. Every note is for itself and yet not for itself; its meaning emerges only in a cosmos, within an order. This relation is simultaneously a uniformity and a disharmony.

As rules, possibilities, and reality in musical games cannot be apprehended and 'read' by means of an abstraction or a rational identification of the notes played, so being becomes manifest only in the musical realization of the playing, in its concrete occurrence.

At this stage, we are left with a single last doubt, the paralipomena to all we have discussed so far, one last nagging question. As early as 9 February 1793, in a letter to his father, Novalis wrote: "I had fallen in love with a girl—please show leniency and forgive my youth. At first, all was proceeding very well, but this passion of mine kept growing so fast that before long it had me completely in its grip. I lacked the strength to resist it. I totally surrendered to it."[48]

On 14 March 1797, Novalis wrote to Friedrich Schlegel, who was back from Thuringen, with the almost apodictic certainty that Sophie had but a few days to live. On 22 March 1797, in Weissenfels, he wrote to Karl Ludwig Woltmann at Jena:

> I have never feared destiny. I have seen it loom over me only in the last three weeks. Night has fallen for me, while I was still in the light of dawn. My grief, like my love, is endless. She has been my obsession for three years... With her I have been separated from everything else, I have almost lost all control over myself. Night has fallen for me...[49]

The abyss becomes more compelling in sorrow. Even pain undergoes a process of *becoming*, is transformed and finally settles into coldness and indifference, which are perhaps even more terrifying than the very pain they replace. Should we regard Novalis's pain only as a

---

48 Novalis, *Schriften*, 4:106, 110.
49 Novalis, *Schriften*, 4:204, 206.

subjective, psychological grief he alone experienced? Is it a biographical datum only? Should we interpret his lament cynically, as if he had merely forgotten all that he had said about the need to go beyond individual beings? Is there no compassion for the suffering of one who would chance the world itself in a game? Are these questions utterly unjustified?

# The Painful Romanticization of Reality: Nerval

## 1) *The Metaphorization of Reality*

On the basis of our observations on Novalis's concept of Romanticism, we shall now turn to an author generally not examined from a philosophical point of view. We will thus complete the arguments discussed so far and exemplify the philosophical aspects of the Romantic movement. As we broach our subject, it is our intention to identify the meaning of a body of writings which, though literary in nature, represents also a record of the fantastic imaging process experienced in a work of art. For the sake of historical clarity, we must first establish what relationship there was between Nerval and the German Romantic tradition. We know for sure that Nerval never read any of Novalis's works, nor was he familiar with the set of problems dealt with by the German author.

Nerval was two years old when, on 29 November 1810, his mother died on the Polish border with Germany. She was buried in Gross-Glogan. Her husband, Dr. Etienne Lamninie, was an army doctor in a local hospital. Nerval translated the first part of *Faust* at 18; ten years later, he traveled to Germany with Dumas; in 1839 he visited Austria, in 1843 the Orient, in 1849 England, and in 1850 he returned to Germany.

On the matter of Nerval's rapport with Germany as his spiritual motherland, the following excerpts speak for themselves: "How wonderful! Following the banks of the Rhine, I have rediscovered my voice and the instruments of my work."[1] In a letter to Francis Wey

---

[1] G. de Nerval, *Correspondance*, ed. A. Béguine and J. Richer (Paris: Gal-

dated 18 June 1854, he wrote: "We are all mad in Germany." In *Sur un carnet de Gérard de Nerval* we find the following note: "Imagine! In Germany they don't think I am insane at all." [2] Nerval was influenced especially by Heine, E.T.A. Hoffman, and Holderlin. His translation of Heine was published in *Revue des Deux Mondes* on 15 July 1848. When he was institutionalized in the "maison municipale de santé" in the faubourg Saint-Denis (from 6 February to 7 March 1853) for a relapse into insanity, Heine was constantly at his bed-side.

We can infer all that Germany represented for Nerval from the initial poetic pages of *Angélique*:

> In 1851, I was passing through Frankfurt. Since I was forced to remain two days in this city, with which I was already familiar, I found no other diversion than to walk through its main streets, which were then crowded with vendors. Roemer square, above all, glittered with a quantity of goods of extraordinary luxury. Not far from there, the fur market displayed an infinity of animal hides, which had arrived from Northern Siberia and from the Caspian Sea. The polar bear, the blue fox, and the ermine were the least expensive curiosities in that unequalled exhibition. Further on, glasses from Bohemia sparkled with a thousand colours, stacked, beribboned, carved, inlaid with gold, all in a beautiful display on benches with cedar shelves, like cut flowers from an unknown paradise. [3]

Our interpretation of Nerval's thought must begin with the long dedication to A. Dumas contained in the introduction to *Les filles du feu*. In connection with this, we must recall that Jules Janis, on 1 March 1841, having heard false rumors of Nerval's death, published an obituary in the *Journal des Débates*. Dumas as well would later write extensively on Nerval, in the 10 December 1853 issue of *Le Mousquetaire*, in his *Causerie avec mes lecteurs*. The piece was occasioned by the publication of Nerval's *El Desdichado*. In his dedication to the French novelist, Nerval refers to both the obituary and

---

limard, 1952), n. 311, letter to G. Bell, dated 3 May 1854; cf. also *Oeuvres*, ed. H. Lemeitre (Paris: Garnier, 1966), 864 n. 3.

[2] *Oeuvres*, 864.

[3] *Oeuvres*, 504–505.

Dumas's article, wondering how he could have deserved such lavish praise. Having overcome the latest attack of his illness, Nerval hoped to be able to come back to earth a reasonable man, as Astolfo did in the *Orlando Furioso* after searching for Orlando's reason on the moon: "But now that I am no longer riding the Hippogriff, and that, in the eyes of mortals, I have recovered what is commonly called reason, let's reason."[4]

In his article, Dumas had described Nerval's personality and abilities, and had advanced the following interpretation of his insanity: "From time to time, when he is quite preoccupied with a piece of work, his imagination, that madcap, drives his reason off momentarily."[5] When the imagination becomes "all-powerful in his dream-ridden and hallucinated mind," then Nerval supposedly undergoes what opium smokers experience. The wandering imagination "drives him into impossible theories and unwritable books."[6]

Dumas writes that Nerval is not only able to describe his journey into insanity, he is also able to convey it with such wonderful images that each one of us wants to live through those adventures and enter the world of chimeras, the oasis of the imagination. Nerval, however, notes Dumas, falls into the arms of melancholy, which becomes his muse, and thus creates works which arouse unrestrainable emotions in his readers. Nerval challenges Dumas's interpretation, stressing that he will speak 'reasonably': "I shall try to explain to you, my dear Dumas, the phenomenon to which you have referred."[7]

At this point we must ask ourselves: What is the subject of Nerval's works? He does not relate fantastic tales or imaginary stories, but what he has lived through:

> Once convinced that I was writing my own story, I began to express all my dreams, all my emotions: I was moved by this love for a fugitive *star* who left me alone in the night of my destiny, I wept, I trembled from the vain apparitions of my sleep.[8]

---

[4] *Oeuvres*, 491; (partial) English translation in S. Rhodes, *Gérard de Nerval* (New York: Philosophical Library, 1951), 357.

[5] *Oeuvres*, 492; Rhodes, 356.

[6] *Oeuvres*, 492; Rhodes, 356.

[7] *Oeuvres*, 493.

[8] *Oeuvres*, 502; Rhodes, 358.

Nerval, then, wants to shed light on his own personal experiences, on the unfolding of his own life-story. This arouses our curiosity. But curiosity for what exactly? Certainly not for the mere sequence of events, but for what he has had to endure, for what continues to pursue him, for what he is subjected to and for which he suffers. His work does not bear the mark of superficial or literary curiosity but is dominated, rather, by existential urgency.

In making the second important point in his rebuttal to Dumas, Nerval also states, as we have already seen, that he set out to 'translate' what befalls him. But in what originary context? This is where the essential element of his 'Romantic' thinking emerges. He depends on a woman to fulfill his destiny; the essence of such a passion must be interpreted, in his work, as the infernal dimension of the unusual which confronts him with this question: Where and how can we entrust ourselves to something which will lead us to safety? His answer: "surrounded by monsters against which I struggled confusedly, I got hold of Ariadne's thread."[9] He turns to a woman for help, a woman who is a symbol of all the women of his existence.

By following that thread, which glows in the dark like a bright indicative trail, Nerval leaves behind the gloomy hollows to conquer the sphere of light ("all my visions have become celestial"). This story, his story, his personal 'divine comedy,' his ascent from hell, from the darkness of pain, becomes the object of his 'translation,' his 'metaphorization' of the world: "Some day I will write about this descent into the netherworld." This story, he readily concedes to Dumas, lacks rationality, but not a foundation: "You will observe that it is not altogether devoid of arguments, although it has always been devoid of logic."[10]

To explicate what he means by 'translating,' 'transposing,' 'metaphorizing' his personal experiences, Nerval adopts a German term, maintaining that his sonnets were "written in a state of *supernatural imagination*, as the Germans would say."[11] Nerval here is consciously challenging idealistic rationalism in its claim that objectivity can be apprehended through the dialectic of reason. He states that his verses, prose, and tales "are not much more obscure than Hegel's metaphysics."

---

[9] *Oeuvres*, 502; Rhodes, 358.

[10] *Oeuvres*, 502.

[11] *Oeuvres*, 503.

His life-story unveils the mysterious reality of an original suffering which has no rational explanations. For this reason, he declares that his sonnets have no legitimacy on logical grounds, and that if they had it, they would lose their appeal: "to explain them, if that were possible, would be to deprive them of their charm."[12]

## 2) Fire, Dreams and the Dialectic of Passion

His introduction to *Les Filles du feu*, dedicated to Dumas, covers other important points. His literature purports to represent his effort to escape the subjective, psychological context of a purely literary activity.

First of all we must grasp fully the implications of the complete title of his works, which include the stories of several women: Angélique, Sylvie, Octavie, Isis, Corilla. The whole title reads: *Les Filles du feu et les Chimères* (1854).

But what fire could this be? Does it ravage or does it purify, enabling us to see something new? Are the chimeras he mentions fantastic figures of dreams or do they disclose a reality, generally not known, which corresponds to Novalis's intention to 'romanticize' the world? Can it be that his program is more than merely literary, in so far as he wants to escape pure fantasy and thus gain a deeper understanding of reality? One year before the publication of *les Filles du feu*, on 21 October 1853, Nerval wrote to his father to let him know of his recovery from the latest nervous breakdown. The fire of his illness had been devastating, burning to ashes his everyday world, where he could no longer find any rest or cling to anything. In his madness he had discovered two realities: the reality of individual beings, and the reality of the directly experienced impulse of being.

A few months later, not only did he set out to write the entire collection of *Les Filles du feu*, he also published, on 10 December 1853, his sonnet *El Desdichado*, where he described himself as a mysterious, inconsolable widower: "I am the dark, widowed, disconsolate one."[13]

In *Les Filles du feu* he included works written earlier; among these, *Sylvie*, which he had written between two stays in mental institutions; it had first appeared in *Revue des Deux Mondes* on 15 August

---

[12] *Oeuvres*, 503.
[13] *Oeuvres*, 693; English translation in Rhodes, 346.

1853. He also included *Octavie*, which had been published in *Le Mous-quetaire*. As for the fire motif in *Octavie*, *Isis* and *Corilla*, critics see it as the symbolization of Mount Vesuvius, which is its pagan meaning, but they relate it to his passions for Sylvie, Angélique, and Jenny Colon. What is, then, this sphere of light he lives in, also defined as "this beautiful dawn, which has always filled me with light, and during its absence I am in the perpetual company of a circle of darkness"?[14]

Nerval's thesis concerns, in the first place, the primacy of passion in the context of which real beings manifest their different and forever changing meaning, while subjecting us to the urgency of their impulse, and, in the second place, the exemplifying theme of the dream.

Love and passion constitute the central motifs of Romanticism and of the 'romanticization' of the world, which determine Nerval's destiny. But the theme of love is connected to the theme of death. He tells us, in fact, that Angélique finds love in her experience of death: "The grief that Angélique felt for his death revealed love to her."[15] Our irremediable separation now points back to a primordial insepa-rability. But then where should we seek reality? Not in just any passion, such as fear, anguish, hate, and envy, but in the passion of love, which seeks unity.

Nerval's theory of the pre-eminence of passion can be summarized in the following manner: it is in passion alone that the body can shine with a silvery glow in the soft outline of a breast, a limb, a stride, and become seductive. Pale and feeble, we tremble when we experience the unattainable, our will deceiving us into believing that we have indeed attained that which is concealed. We drink our life-giving force from a cup made invisible by its transparency, a cup we find refreshing despite the burning passion it holds, a passion that springs forth from a painless wound and pulsates in the veins of life announcing itself as a 'gay science'.

It is then that the process of metamorphosis sets in, and the whole of life, including all that announces itself in it, is at stake. The pores of nature open up to disclose, through the senses, the secret which reason pursues in vain. In what comes forth from this, there springs up life, only to conceal itself later in graves. Life and death, intimate-

[14] *Oeuvres*, 527.
[15] *Oeuvres*, 527.

ly connected, shed light on each other, and the ineluctability of time, which binds together past, present, and future, is shattered. The signs that indicate such a transposition rise to the level of emblems of life and language at the primordial stage. On the threshold of metaphor angels with unsheathed swords stand in vigilance so that nothing that is not pure may surreptitiously cross it.

Nerval 'metaphorizes' reality in order to identify its deep structure, which reveals itself in the compelling impulse of the abyss of passion, as a function of which, in the here and now, the constantly changing meaning of reality manifests itself. Nerval struggles for this strange event, for the romanticization of the world, in Novalis's sense. We may recall, on this point, Schlegel's words in *Lucinde*: "Create, discover, transform, and retain the world in its eternal forms in the perpetual variation of new marriages and divorces. Veil and bind the spirit in the letter. The real letter is all-powerful; it's the true magic wand. It is the letter with which the irresistible will of that great magician, Fantasy, touches the sublime chaos of all-encompassing nature, touches it and calls the infinite word to light, the word that is an image and a mirror of the divine spirit, and that mortals call the universe."[16]

The presupposition of the process at the basis of Nerval's thinking consists of the separation of reality into two distinct levels and of the recognition of the fact that we feel constantly urged to metaphorize the meaning of beings in the light of what is originary. That is what Nerval means when he says that the world of dreams is an exemplification of the context in which, without a rational structure but intimately connected nevertheless, a world of phenomena appears. In the third chapter of *Aurélia* he states: "Here began for me what I shall call the overflowing of the dream into real life."[17]

How are the two worlds, of dreams and reality, different for Nerval? The world of dreams is not grounded in reason, and, for that reason, it is reduced by rationalism to a mere illusion: "My actions were apparently insensate because they were subject to what, according to human reason, is called illusion."[18] He says: "From that mo-

---

[16] F. Schlegel, *Lucinde and the Fragments*, tr. P. Firchow (Minneapolis: Univ. of Minnesota Press, 1971), 58.

[17] *Oeuvres*, 760; English translation by R. Aldington, *Aurelia* [contains also *Sylvie* and selections from other works] (London: Chatto & Windus, 1932), 6.

[18] *Oeuvres*, 760; Aldington, 6.

ment on, everything at times had a double aspect."[19] The world of dreams Nerval speaks of is neither subjective nor psychological in nature; it is, rather, the experience of a groundless, mysterious reality which comes to presence and on account of which one suffers "in certain serious moments of life,"[20] when the difference between the rational world and the nonrational one, between what is derivable and what is underivable, imposes itself on us.

Critics have stressed that the motif of the meaning of dreams has become central for several literary movements, and that it is a matter of an "interprètation visionnaire et onirique"[21] of poetry seen as a subjective creative process. That assessment, however, misinterprets the deeper existential meaning of the dream in Nerval, for whom it is a matter of exemplifying how a manifestation which is impossible to legitimize rationally imposes itself on us. When we admit, in our everyday life, the presence of what cannot be legitimized, as in dreams, we become dizzy, we lose our balance: "At the same time I threw off my earthly garments and scattered them about me."[22]

What we have before us is an attempt to exemplify the experience of a difference, namely the difference made by the urgings of an appeal which obliges us to transpose the meaning of all beings into a realm far more originary than that of rationality: "Then I felt a shudder go through me. Regret for the earth and those I loved there seized on my heart, and I made such earnest supplication within me to the Spirit attracting me that it seemed to me that I returned to mankind."[23]

These words are not reducible to mysticism, or to the problematics of literature and fantasy, because they represent an attempt to explain his theory of the dual nature of reality. Nerval's concerns, then, are not primarily literary. The distinction between, and the identification of, dream and reality must be symbolic of the presence and urgings of the abyss. We recall that a passage from a letter addressed to Dr. Blanche, dated 15 July 1854, reads: "I ... who have difficulty in distinguishing dreams from reality."[24]

---

[19] *Oeuvres*, 760; Aldington, 6.
[20] *Oeuvres*, 760; Aldington, 6.
[21] *Oeuvres*, 760 n. 1.
[22] *Oeuvres*, 760; Aldington, 6.
[23] *Oeuvres*, 760–761; Aldington, 6.
[24] *Correspondance*, n. 331, in *Oeuvres*, 865 n.

What tensions reveal the abyss, what dialectic of love? In a letter to *Aurélia*, Nerval writes: "We now have to guard against one thing, and that is the lassitude which follows every violent tension, every super-human effort. For one who has only a moderate desire, success is a supreme joy which brings out all the other human faculties. It is a luminous point in existence which soon grows pale and flickers out." [25]

According to Nerval, our existence is played out in the passion of love; that which is compelling appears in the here and now of this passion. Only the rigidity of abstraction can speak of the absolute, since it manifests itself primarily in the dialectic of thought.

What is the drama of Aurélia? It is the drama of Romantic thought as we find it in Novalis's project; it is not a mystifying and cabalistic statement. The tragedy of having lived without ever know-ing any compassion, of having failed to find a way to identify reality is what finally led Nerval to commit suicide. He was found hanging from a street lamp; he had with him the proofs of *Aurélia*. This romanticization of the world, this suffering described in the most minute detail, must not be interpreted as the pain of a man afflicted by a mental disorder, but as a profoundly meaningful existential experience which goes beyond the subjective destiny of a single man.

The tragedy touches not just *a* man, but *the* man who not only saw and theorized, but also passionately experienced the dual nature of reality. The story he relates is that of a 'lunatic,' a term which indicates a man who lives, as Nerval himself specified, in a 'monde intermédiare,' halfway between the sun and the darkness of space, between the luminosity of that which is originary and the blackness of an earthly, historical existence. Life in the *lunar* glow is a useless attempt to mitigate the discrepancy between reality and the shadow in our inexorable existence.

The link between these two worlds finds expression in the *lan-guage* of the two lovers. Its function and originary character can be found in the letters to *Aurélia*, where we come across a thesis which at first seems absurd and contradictory: "Letters mean something only to cold lovers and to happy lovers." [26]

What does the author mean by that statement? Can it be that he

---

[25] *Oeuvres*, 851; Aldington, 64.
[26] *Oeuvres*, 832.

differentiates between the *written* word and the *spoken* word? Why
does he deal with passion in the context of the *Word*? What is called
into play in the language of passion?

The statement just quoted is followed in the text by what appears
to be an elucidation: "In conversations we admit disorder and inco-
herence, but written sentences become eternal witnesses."[27]

Let us now see why letters are valid only for cold lovers. For
those who no longer love each other, the written word is like a
tombstone on the passion that once was. The game is no more: Coldness has replaced the warmth of their touch; they have become rigid
in their movement. A tombstone can only be inscribed with an epi-
taph. But the happy lover also seeks uselessly to preserve in the written
word what he has attained. We are here before the illusion of Ovid,
who, at the beginning of the *Metamorphoses*, thinks that in the written
word he has carved out his message and preserved it for eternity.

The cold despair of a love which is no longer and the impetuous
happiness of a fulfilled love believe that the written word can preserve passion. However, museums, histories of literature, and archaeo-
logical collections, all bearing testimony to what once was, are full of
words and rigid testimonies, which are waiting to be exorcized. That
gives meaning to Nerval's exclamation in *Aurélia*: "How I wish that
I could destroy everything I have written you."[28]

The case of the spoken word is completely different: It involves
the passionate process. Nothing is fixed; everything is still suspended
and doubtful, in a state of contradiction and becoming, between hope
and the fear of disillusionment. The lover, through the word, tries to
conquer a new world and free a new future from death. In the
language of passion everything is confusing and incoherent, and
contradictions are possible and bear vivid testimony to passionateness.
In the spoken word something that urges us, that is compelling and
alive, reveals itself to us.

## 3) The Dialectic of Passion

The initial problem of Nerval's romanticism is not the problem of
individual beings but passionateness, as a function of which reality

---

[27] *Oeuvres*, 832.
[28] *Oeuvres*, 832.

manifests its different meanings. What we are dealing with here is the dialectic of love which, as it flourishes and perishes, animates and enlightens reality. Nerval analyzes love in its metaphorical reality: "A difficult and complicated struggle was necessary for a love like mine. Such an indefatigable passion needed a remarkable resistance. [. . .] this dumb persistent activity ... ardent as a Spanish passion, supple as Italian love."[29] The dialectic of existence is therefore a continuous dramatic search. It is an urging which discloses the many colors of reality and gives us hope, while the uncertainty of the latter causes us to fall back into melancholy, into the fear that the flame may die out.

To underestimate this experience, to analyze it in abstract terms, is to reject reality: "Thought is congealed when it is translated into sentences, and the sweetest emotions of love resemble then the dried flowers we press between the pages of a book to preserve them better."[30] Nerval is not concerned with psychological experiences; he wants to describe the struggle to distinguish the ordinary from the originary, to decipher reality, to assert the importance of love in relation to other passions. Since it opens up a wider spectrum of possibilities, love affirms the value and the insignificance of reality at every instant. The pre-eminence of love is thereby affirmed, for all the other passions are rooted in it; they all branch out from love to form the forest in which we live. Now, in order to view this land-scape, we need the wind of passion which rises and abates with a rhythm like the one of the seasons, causing flowers to bloom and to wither away. Such a dialectic is metaphorical in nature; it exorcizes female characters as it would the Thessalian sorceresses whom man yearns to meet in his dreams, at the cost of giving up his own heart. Each of these women speaks a different language: "oh!—she said—I can also speak differently. And suddenly she started to speak a lan-guage I have never heard before. She spoke sonorous and guttural syllables with enchanting trills, perhaps in a primitive language; Hebrew, Syriac, I don't know."[31]

Thus Nerval admits that he is not destined to eternal suffering, and neither does he aspire to power and fame, but to the experience

---

[29] *Oeuvres*, 849; Aldington, 63.
[30] *Oeuvres*, 847.
[31] *Oeuvres*, 644.

of that primordial reality. In fact, in his first letter to Aurélia he states: "In my head there is a storm of thoughts that are blinding me. There are years of dreams, of projects, of anxieties that now would like to find expression in a sentence, in a word."[32]

The dialectic of passionate language exorcizes the activities of the senses as well as what they manifest, namely the contemporary emergence of something new and hence also of death as the perishing away of a period of time:

Death!... Sometimes I dreamed that she would wait for me smiling by the bed of a woman I adored, after the happiness, after the intoxication, and that she would say: 'Come, young man, you have received your entire share of joy in this world. Now come to sleep, come to rest in my arms. I am not beautiful, but I am good and I save, and I do not give pleasure but eternal calm.'[33]

At this point we should ask ourselves whether pain does not have pre-eminence over joy. Pain draws out its substance from the darkness of the netherworld and is connected, in an unknowable way, with man's blood, his sensuality, and his primordial cry. From those hollows, from that connection emerges the timid, hesitant figure of a woman enveloped in her modesty, her eyes sparkling, her smile bewitching, as the smile Sappho described, in the poem dedicated to Venus, on the lips of the lover who, like a god, approaches his beloved and intoxicated with joy, hears not words but her silvery laugh. From the subterranean world of pain springs the multiplicity of reality—fragments of life, worlds, memories, embraces. Is this the destiny announced in *Aurélia* and sought for and outlined in *En marge d'Aurélia*? "You are not like other women for me. I can renounce jealousy, I can sacrifice my patriotism, but I cannot do without the secret rights of my heart over another."[34] Soon after Nerval writes: "In the concessions to which I am driven by my love for you, I willingly give up my pride as a man, my pretensions as a lover, but do show me a little pity for my suffering, for this terrible exaltation,

[32] *Oeuvres*, 832.
[33] *Oeuvres*, 642.
[34] *Oeuvres*, 642.

the responsibility for which I do not recognize as always mine."[35]

We have, then, the primacy of what appears within passion and of what we give up for its sake. On the crest of the rising and falling waves, on the shores of the various situations, on the iridescent foam of the billows, our anguish takes shape. All these waves come from afar, offering us a glimmer of the superficial as well as the profound, spreading a silvery glow on the beach if the moon shines high in the sky. Passion needs substances to feed on; it needs darkness and confusion brought up from below as waves bring pebbles and refuse on a beach. It is then that passions arise: pleasure and pain, fear and hope, envy and dedication: "I say to myself, in the love that I have for you, there is too much past that there should not be much future."[36]

What is, then, the principal concern in Nerval's writings? It is the romantic element, its coming to presence; more specifically, it is the sphere of light which he calls his illness:

> Following them, I shall try to describe the impressions of a long illness which took place wholly in the mysterious places of my spirit. I do not know why I use the word 'illness', for in regard to myself I never felt better. Sometimes I felt my strength and activity doubled; I seemed to know and understand everything; my imagination gave me infinite delight. Must I regret having lost them by recovering what men call reason?[37]

Nerval, then, wants to metaphorize the impressions he received while undergoing an experience that the rest of the world terms insanity; he must do that, since the experiences undergone in the intimacy of our soul, if transferred unaltered to the rational world, appear absurd. Nerval's secret remains inexplicable, since the process of self-legitimization in language can only be identified in the instant it occurs. Is this an illusory process? Is a reality which manifests itself in madness the only reality which will guarantee that we will not stop at concrete beings, that we will be able to go beyond them? But then to what should we entrust ourselves? To the experience of the contra-

---

[35] *Oeuvres*, 842–843.
[36] *Oeuvres*, 834.
[37] *Oeuvres*, 753–754; Aldington, 1–2.

diction between reality and unreality, between pleasure and pain. In the course of this experience, the shell enclosing concrete beings is shattered and with it the illusion we need in our lives to drive us on, beyond the beings themselves. In this shattered illusion, the presence of something beyond beings glows and makes itself manifest.

In *Sylvie* Nerval writes: "Illusions fall one by one, like the husks of a fruit, and the fruit is experience. Its taste is bitter, yet there is something sharp about it which is tonic—forgive this old-fashioned style."[38]

Dumas, in his article on Nerval, explains that when the imagination takes over, its visions and representations are expressed in "impossible theories and unwritable books."[39] Nerval's goal, however, is not to realize his own subjective imagination but to decipher what we all suffer and enjoy in order to apprehend his own more profound identity. In attempting this, Nerval experiences the objectivity which takes possession of us, makes it possible for us to find the right words, helps us identify the essence of other men, and forces us to reject all forms of arbitrariness. Overcome by images that cannot be legitimized by reason, by impossible projects, Nerval tries to live his life.

Illusion, then, is necessary to our lives in order for us to decipher reality. And illusion, here, is to be taken as Leaopardi understood it, as *il-ludere*, to play for the stake of life in a double sense—to actualize in the game the rules forced upon us and to make manifest the possibilities of existence. Hence the significance of the game of language referred to by Novalis, and the importance of the *expériences* stressed by Nerval, here understood as '*ex periculo ire*', meaning to experience one's own historicity. Nerval experienced this, as evidenced by the poem where he extols Posillipo, or when he walked the alleys of Naples where the colorful washing, hung outside to dry, stretching from window to window high above,—with its variety of reds, purples and yellows—excited his illusions.

The significance of *Lettres à Aurélia*, where Nerval expressed all his doubts, hopes, and disillusionments, becomes clear once we understand that its goal is to show love as intimately connected with language, as an existential problem that we can fully grasp if we insist on its variations. It is the metaphorical power of reality that discloses

---

[38] *Oeuvres*, 624; Aldington, 109.
[39] *Oeuvres*, 492.

its dual nature, which contrasts with the single dimension of the rational world, forever and uselessly intent on apprehending, through dialectic, the meaning of abstract, fossilized beings. The primordial aspect of language appears in a lunar world, in a place between the earth and the sun; in its context, light and darkness are not as violent and painful as they appear to be in the rational world, lit by the sun.

The pre-eminence given by Nerval to love bears testimony to his insight into the essence of things and makes the meaning of his thesis comprehensible to all: "But for those hearts which are more profoundly in love, the excess of emotion mixes together for an instant all the resources of life. Their agitation is great, their confusion profound, and their heads bow, trembling, as if under the breath of God."[40]

Where and how are we to experience our own loss of reason? In his writings, Nerval has answered our query by means of the symbols of doubt, the questioning of the essence of the beloved, and the passion of perceptible signs. From this derives the power of vigilant doubt because it chisels out the reality of life from the dryness of abstract reality.

Romantic reality, into which reason sinks and finally loses itself, can manifest itself in the isolation of a quiet afternoon with the sudden appearance of blasts of wind. Then, we are astonished to find a reality in the wave of passion, a metamorphosis in the rustling of the leaves; and it frightens us because it makes manifest a reality which differs from the one we experienced the day before. The madman Nerval speaks of trembling, clutches the hand which someone has silently offered him, and then reality and passion burn in the light contact of the palms of two hands, which are carved with the signs of destiny.

---

[40] *Oeuvres*, 851.

# The Lament of *Ecclesiastes*

## 1) *The New Task*

*On the Sublime,* Longinus's text, and our reflections on the non-derivability of the *phonai* have returned us to the originary realm of our existence: language. The reality of passions already bursts forth in the *phonai,* in the semantic suggestions which constitute the first elements of language, namely, of the expressions of the need to respond to the urgency in the call from the abyss of our reality. Longinus teaches us that inauthentic passions are those which do not correspond to *kairós,* to the instant which determines our situation. But how do we identify *kairós*? Certainly not through abstract rational thinking, for it is the immediacy of passionate experience that generates the ethical question of the right attitude and hence of our ethical nature.

Our life as communicative beings with others and with ourselves, our inner and outer dialogue, constitutes a continuous metaphorical response to the pressing needs of existence:

> Our entire life as communicative beings (even our dialogue with ourselves) is always a metaphor; it is a continuous and inevitable succession of 'figurative modes of expressions' and symbols through which we attempt to master our passions. We are always, in every one of our expressions, the source and the destination of 'messages' and 'signals' in which we seek and from which we hope to receive true 'interpretations.' Our life is a 'forest' of metaphors and symbols amongst which it is difficult to clear our path because ambiguity is a constant threat, the 'codes' are ignored or subverted, and communication is 'ambushed.'[1]

---

[1] Letter to the author by Cesare Vasoli, dated 15 May 1988.

Our reflections on the originary nature of phonetic signs—not to be interpreted as sounds (*psophoi*) to which we surreptitiously assign a meaning—led us to the awareness that all that becomes manifest through the senses appears through organs, the instruments of a groundless reality we must respond to, thereby disclosing the scenes of our world.

Our meditations have pointed to the underivable structure of that which appears through the senses. We have made a concerted effort to emphasize the originary passionate nature of that which appears. Therefore, we will devote our attention, after having examined the structure of sounds, to the question of language. How can we explain the difference, and the complexity of *logos* as compared to *phonê?*

We must now identify the phenomena by virtue of which our world is revealed to us so that we may disclose the realm and the meaning of primordial passion. No *phonê*, no sensory perception hovers isolated in mid-air, in abstract, rarefied space. On the contrary, it becomes crystallized in various situations, in the signification of individual beings which appear within an ordered system in accordance with principles of measure. There arises a *kosmos* that is in no way a human creation, but which dawns and sets in a temporal *phyein* to the rhythm of the warning signals of an underivable absolute.

The world is exorcized by the *phonai* in so far as it is precisely through these sounds that phenomena, understood as perceptible presences, take on the shapes of significant objects which are not revealed through a mere reflection, through the careful and circumspect allusion referred to, for example, by Herder in his essay on the origins of language.

In the *phonai*, these perceptible indicative signs emerge not as functions of individual beings but rather from the call of the abyss, whose organs are our senses. It is precisely through the senses that our theater, our *theorein* raises its curtain. Moreover, the *phonai* themselves acquire different meanings in different languages. This is not valid only for indicative *phonai*, but for all indications of the senses: odors, tastes, colors, all tactile sensations, movements and therefore the dance with its varying rhythm. Consequently, when an invading population bursts into an ordered system and disrupts the environmental stimuli of a community, it destroys that world, that *kosmos*. This brought about the tragic, painful demise of the Indian communities of North and South America, for example, at the hands of European invaders. The misunderstanding of indicative signs, which appear strange and meaningless to the invader, initiates the destruction of indigenous populations. The invader can no longer rely on sensory perceptions, for they take on unexpected meanings in different historical situations. Different stages make for radical changes of sets and scenes, and in their process of becoming we must search for the authentic code that will enable us to disclose and simultaneously seal each era of history.

This realization obliges us to acknowledge a fundamental truth: we are swimming in a sea of *phonai* and myriad sensory signals in a desperate attempt to reach an island offered to us by destiny so that we may find there our peaceable epoch.

"When we leaf through, even distractedly, any compendium on phonetics [...] we are surprised to discover their richness and variety."[2] Fonagy stresses the fact that each element of *phonai* "has a different tone-colour that can be 'light' or 'dark', for example. Consonants seem to acquire a certain consistency; they can be 'hard' or 'soft', and in particular instances they are perceived even as 'moist'."[3]

In dealing even with the phonetic elements alone, we must already concede to their variety of timbre which, in turn, implies variety of meaning. We cannot stress sufficiently enough the importance of the polysemous character of the *phonai*:

> Whenever all the inner vibrations of our heartstrings—the trembling ones of joy, the tempestuous ones of delight, the rapidly beating pulse of all-consuming adoration,—when all these burst apart with *one* outcry the language of words, as the *grave* of the inner frenzy of heart:—then they go forth under a strage sky, amidst the vibrations of blessed harpstrings, in transfigured beauty as if in another life beyond this one, and celebrate as angelic figures their resurrection.[4]

---

[2] Ivan Fonagy, *Die Metaphern in der Phonetyk. Beitrag zur Entwicklungsgeschichte des wissenschaftlichen Denkens* (The Hague: Mouton, 1963), 11.

[3] Ibid.

[4] Wilhelm Heinrich Wackenroder, *Phantasien über die Kunst für Freunde der Kunst*, ed. L. Tieck (Berlin-Stuttgart: Spemann, 1885), 70; English translation M.H. Schubert, *Fantasies on Art for Friends of Art*, in *Confessions and Fantasies* (University Park and London: The Pennsylvania State Univ. Press, 1971), 190–191.

The elements of language are not metaphors merely in the sense that a certain meaning is transferred onto meaningless phenomena that are mechanically explained. Rather, they constitute already an originary revelation of the forces that exhort us here and now and herald the elements of our world.

On this subject we shall cite another passage in Wackenroder's treatise, which shows the indicative nature of phonetic elements, whose meaning is underivable through a rational process:

> Now, when the subtle reasoners ask: where, actually, the center of this art is to be found, where its true meaning and its soul lie hidden, where all its varied manifestations are held together?—then I cannot explain or demonstrate it to them. Whoever wants to discover with the divining-rod of the investigating intellect that which can only be felt from within will perpetually discover only thoughts about emotion and not emotion itself. [. . .] —He who undermines the most beautiful and most holy things in the realm of the spirit with his 'Why?' and with relentless searching for Purpose and Cause, is actually not concerned with the beauty and divinity of the things themselves but with his algebra.[5]

Only by taking as our point of departure the experience of the passionate nature of *psophoy* can we hope for the chance to find Ariadne's thread, our guide through the labyrinth of the interpretation of the world. Let us recall the last assumption of Romanticism:

> The *psophoy* wave or note was originally a crude material in which uncivilized peoples strove to express their undeveloped emotions. When their souls were deeply shaken, they also shook the surrounding air with screaming and the beating of drums, as if to bring the external world into balance with their inner spiritual excitation.[6]

Originary emotion is passionately experienced through the indicative signs of the senses within the limits of pleasure and pain. We exist and function in a passionately experienced world granted to us by

---

[5] Wackenroder 70; Schubert, 190.
[6] Wackenroder, 67; Schubert, 188.

signs that direct us and caution us. The act of appearance of these signs, which bind us and compel us, marks the beginning of the game that discloses our possibilities. The confrontation with the reality of such originary experience constitutes the act that generates our world.

We have so far devoted our attention to the issue of the underivedness of phonetic elements. Now, leaving aside the problem of language, we shall study a text grounded on the consideration of the sorrow of existence as experienced in various situations.

One of the first canonical texts in the history of Western culture is the *Book of Ecclesiastes.*

Our task is to stress the need for a distinction between two different paradigms concerned with the revelation of the being of individual beings: one based on rational, abstract, ahistorical presuppositions, and another one based on the story, the *fabula,* the narrated account of our experience which forces us to seek out the commitments we must live up to in order to realize our existence. All that the author in the *Book of Ecclesiastes* narrates is presented to us by means of signs that emerge from specific situations, from particular experiences which appear within the coordinates of pleasure and pain. The stories are born of the experience of seeking out the order in which all existing beings attempt to find their points of reference.

## 2) Lament and Ashes

Ecclesiastes is the Greek Septuagint translation of the Hebrew term Qoheleth, the name of the author which appears frequently in the text. [7] The different theses contained in the text give rise to the difficulties incurred by the translators in interpreting its meaning. Some examples: the celebration of existential joy[8] *vis-à-vis* the thesis on the inherent sorrow of existence;[9] the recognition[10] and the negation of the value of knowledge.[11] Hence the question asked by various exegetes: Could these constitute different theses advanced by different authors contradicting each other? Could this be an example

---

[7] I, 1, 2, 12; VII, 27; XII, 8–10.

[8] II, 24; III, 12.

[9] II, 2; VII, 2–5.

[10] II, 13; VII, 19; IX, 6.

[11] I, 17, 18; II, 15, 19.

of profound skepticism and pessimism? Do the theses contrast with
the original Hebrew tradition? It is generally believed that the text
was written during the second or third century before Christ. Of the
classical commentators we choose to mention only Saint Jerome[12]
and Saint Bonaventure.[13]

It has been indicated that the language used by Qoheleth is not
altogether the Hebrew characteristic of the Prophets: a close analysis
of the text points to expressions, words and syntactical structures of
Aramaic derivation. Scholars have admitted that Qoheleth's anxious
quest, unlike Saint Augustine's, *does not* culminate in a revelation.
His fundamental thesis is that no human effort, no human activity
can presuppose a transcendental religious compensation. Biblical
scholars have advanced the hypothesis that the text was written under
the influence of Hellenistic trends, and consequently that the work is
a document attesting to attitudes of skepticism towards the value of
human activity and human existence.

To deny that this text differs radically from the teachings of the
Old Testament is to refuse to see it for what it is. The God of *Ecclesiastes* is an impersonal god, a *Deus absconditus* who, unlike the God
conceived by Nicholas of Cusa, does not reveal himself to us. Needless to say, the text is exploited by Christianity as evidence of the
tragedy of human existence and, therefore, as a legitimation of man's
hope for transcendence into another kingdom.

Access to this text is immediately precluded by an interpretation
based on the well-known maxim, *Vanitas vanitatum*, which commonly heads it. The Hebrew word for *vanitas* is *abel*, the name of
Adam's second son.[14] Its lexical possibilities are the following: wind,
breath, transience, nothingness. When used in its adverbial form it
means 'in vain.' What meaning does the Vulgate ascribe to the term
*vanitas?* Vanity is a human attitude generated by the belief in what
can elicit an external, superficial recognition, devoid of value. It
implies a negative judgement. In our text, such judgement is not
arrived at through theoretical, logical arguments, but is rather the

---

[12] S. Hieronymi Presbyteri, *Opera*, pars I, 1, in Corpus Christianorum, Series
Latina, LXXII (Turnholti: Brepols, 1959), 249ff.

[13] S. Bonaventurae, *Opera Omnia* (Claras Aquas: Quaracchi, 1883), vol. VI.

[14] Genesis, 4, 2.

result of the analysis of situations specific to man. The interpretation of our text must therefore be based on these.

What method does our author use to convey his thoughts? He describes indicative situations which bear the markings of pain and pleasure. These experiences never issue from abstract, metaphysical reflections, but rather from the effort to see and to know in accordance with the dictates of the heart.

> To my heart I speak
> I say to him
> - Oh, what greatness!
>
> . . . .
> I, the heart that has seen
> The greatest wisdom
> That has experienced all knowledge
> I, the heart who thought himself
> The master of wisdom
> Who penetrated amongst passions
> And discerned follies
> But all was empty breath.[15]

The heart is here the source of life, of the experience and passion of the inspiring and expiring process which heralds forth reality with all its lights and shadows, with its joys and sorrows, with all its myriad mutable meanings.

This is the kind of phenomenology that does not cling to that which appears. It allows for phenomena to develop and evolve without fixing them into abstract forms. It allows them to unfold within the coordinates of pain and pleasure.

Hence the Ecclesiastes states:

> Come I say to my heart
> Let joy inebriate you
> Let happiness appear.[16]

---

[15] *Qohélet o l'Ecclesiaste*, ed. G. Ceronetti (Torino: Einaudi, 1988), 1:16–17. The reader is warned that, given the role of close textual analysis in Grassi's philosophical arguments, we have translated all quotations directly from this Italian edition of the Book of Ecclesiastes (translators' note).

[16] *Qoholét o l'Ecclesiaste*, 2:1.

His method here constitutes the choice of a path (*odós*) that will lead him to existential experiences:

> With a vigilant heart
> . . .
> With wisdom as my guide
> I would immerse myself in folly
> In the hope of discovering
> That in which consists
> The happiness of the sons of men.[17]

What exactly is this method of the heart? It is certainly not a rational method. It buries its roots in the heart, the life-giving organ. Must we discover then, in the experience of existence, the nonbeing of beings? In any case—if we want to consider it a philosophy—it is a method in no way related to any aspect of Platonism. For our author the point of departure is always his own wisdom, his own quest. He even prides himself on having reached his goal:

> Heart of the wise man
> All things done and done again under the sun
> Have I traversed and explored
> A grievous affliction this
> That God has put on man
> To torment him.[18]

The starting point of this phenomenology is the senses, the organs through which the abyss discloses itself to us and to which we remain forever bound. And yet our author begins to wonder about the possibility that knowledge might lead to something more, that it might deliver us from our destiny, our death.

> But I also know that there is
> One destiny, one for all
> And in my heart I say
> Such is the destiny of a fool
> And such is mine own
> . . .

---

[17] *Qoholét o l'Ecclesiaste*, 2:3.
[18] *Qoholét o l'Ecclesiaste*, 1:13.

Neither of the wise man nor of the fool
Will memory remain in time
Soon in days to come
All will be forgotten
Wise man and fool
Death will have them both.[19]

In the context of the Platonic tradition, knowledge leads us beyond the limits of historical time, beyond sensory manifestation, and the process of rational abstraction is a process of deliverance. The fact that our text does not specify right at its inception the role of reason is an indication of the distance separating the *Book of Ecclesiastes* from the Platonic tradition.

Our heart constantly reminds us of the importance of our enjoyment of things, it goes beyond them, it never drowns in them, for in so doing it would ignore their transience. This is precisely what our text continuously points out. With regard to this, the following two passages are particularly significant:

Nothing my eyes wished to see
Was denied them
And never was my heart restrained
In his attempt to draw happiness
From all my suffering
And to seek a better
Destiny with grievous effort
Turning to look at
All I have done

Hands of mine exhausted
Effort expended in doing.[20]

All that the eyes can see never quenches their
thirst for seeing
All that the ears can hear never quenches their
thirst for hearing.[21]

---

[19] *Qohölét o l'Ecclesiaste*, 2:14–16.
[20] *Qohölét o l'Ecclesiaste*, 2:10–11.
[21] *Qohölét o l'Ecclesiaste*, 1:8.

The meaning of the text and the consequences the author derives from it imply a distance from everyday occurrences, from the momentariness of the instant:

> Sweet is the light of day
> And the eyes are made happy
> By the sight of the sun
> . . .
> Young man enjoy your youth
> Go where your heart leads you
> Go where your eyes take you
> . . .
> And cast away torment from your heart.[22]

The author emphasizes the eagerness, the impulse of the senses towards individual beings because they are the instruments of the abyss: they are phenomena with changing meanings, the becoming of the rhythm of time, logical underivedness, transience of reality. Well then, how can we possibly avoid speaking of the vanity of the appearances that we are constantly confronted with?

Yielding to our senses and to our passions in order to attain knowledge, as Qoheleth tells us,[23] means following the sensory directions of the organs of the abyss. Devoting ourselves to all our experiences constitutes our desperate attempt to discover a signal, an indication. And this is Qoheleth's conclusion:

> What will be has already been
> What will be done has already been done
> What is new is what is not.[24]

Any interest whatsoever in history, in the succession of events, and our hopes for new possibilities vanish completely. Reality is always the same; passions lose their meaning; the fear of the future and the hope in what will occur are senseless. The repetition of sameness conquers all. Passions are ephemeral and never new, neither joys nor sorrows. All is sameness:

---

[22] *Qoholét o l'Ecclesiaste,* 11:7–10.
[23] *Qoholét o l'Ecclesiaste,* 2:10.
[24] *Qoholét o l'Ecclesiaste,* 1:9.

> The sun rises
> The sun sets
> It returns to its place
> And rises there again.
> Blowing towards the South and veering to-
> wards the North
> The wind circles round and round
> And turns back to start again its cycle.[25]

What, then, is the object of *theorein*, of our seeing and knowing?

> And I applied myself to investigate
> As a wise man the follies and the passions.[26]

In abstraction, in what lies beyond the confines of time and place, there exists no passion. But then what wisdom is there to talk about? In the realm of an illusion that dissolves all aspects of extra-temporality, where can we possibly search for the real stage of our theater? How can we possibly find the curtain of such stage? What means do we have to raise it?

> Light surpasses darkness
> He who is wise has eyes in his head
> He who is not walks in darkness.[27]

Wisdom is light, it is one with seeing. Well then, are not the senses, in drawing us into the game, the instruments of illusion? Do they not ensnare us in the game, do they not illude us? Why try to raise other curtains to discover other scenes? Denying our senses means sinking into darkness, into silence.

> The living know that they will die
> The dead know nothing at all
> Compensations they have none
> They no longer exist in memory.[28]

---

[25] *Qoholét o l'Ecclesiaste*, 1:5–6.
[26] *Qoholét o l'Ecclesiaste*, 2:12.
[27] *Qoholét o l'Ecclesiaste*, 2:13–14.
[28] *Qoholét o l'Ecclesiaste*, 9:5.

Metamorphosis performs through metaphor: on the stage of death beyond history there are no encounters. We walk among Elysian phantoms of wind and smoke. Better to stop a moment on the shore of Acheron; the boatman is in no hurry, and he knows we will get on again. Silence. In the cave abeyance drips down from the rocks, breath condenses, everything becomes slippery. Why utter another word? Why speak at all another word, even the important last word to someone we know?

> All that your hand
> Is able to do
> Do it until your strength fails you
> For there is no doing
> No inventing
> No thinking
> No knowing
> In the Realm of the Dead where you are bound.[29]

And so we leave the stage, the actor's part done. Another play will have another protagonist. Before stepping off the set you want to say one more word, a word that is yours alone. But what's the point! The wind of time will whirl it in the hollows of a senseless cycle. And who will exorcize your desire to speak, who will deliver it from death? The remembrance of time past has no longer the strength of nostalgia, for you know it is an illusion and it is foolish to believe in it:

> Their love, their hate, their ardor
> All vanished
> Traces of them
> Are no more, will be no more
> In all that happens under the sun.[30]

Both the present and the past escape our understanding. The touch that seeks something to cling to will not find it. The touch is the instrument of an activity, of an *ergon* that forsakes us. Nothing speaks, nothing is expressed, no signals come from the organ that was and is no more. On the stage we tell each other that we share a

---

[29] *Qoh*o*lét o l'Ecclesiaste*, 9:10.
[30] *Qoholét o l'Ecclesiaste*, 9:6.

common destiny, but what we have in common is merely the echo of a lost oneness. The harmony that poured forth as we played the instrument of our existence is destroyed in an instant, and in that instant we are thrust out of the system, we can no longer play our odds in the game of life.

Is it not indeed tragically peculiar of us to want to know, to insist on speaking even at the very moment that shatters our interest in the experience of a game whose odds are always the same? If everything is a constant return to ashes, why blow again on the glowing embers and sit by them just to see the flames that cast changing shadows on the wall?

## 3) The Word We Cannot Hear

What message does the Ecclesiastes himself leave for us? How can we summarize all that we have stated, in the course of our discussion, about the underivedness of originary signs? Ecclesiastes is concerned with the question of the realization of our existence, he explores the futile efforts inherent in it and defines it as an activity undergoing a constant process of transformation caused by the relentless gusting of the winds of time. According to Ecclesiastes, we try with all our strength to remain on the stage of our life, to grasp the meaning of the landscapes painted on the flimsy gauze stretched over moveable flats: images of beaches and cities, the backgrounds necessary to the unfolding of our history. Formulating questions based on these images, to which we cling so desperately, is an act of illusion. Ecclesiastes comes to this unavoidable realization:

> Neither of the wise man nor of the fool
> Will memory remain in time
> Soon in days to come
> All will be forgotten
> Wise man and fool
> Death will have them both.[31]

All that is available to us, then, must be burned in an instant to light up our night, to flicker in the glowing circle of a momentary horizon that marks the beginning of the world of darkness beyond.

---

[31] *Qohôlét o l'Ecclesiaste,* 2:16.

What is the sense of wisdom, of its history, of human events? Let us try now to identify the nature of the existential disillusionment of Ecclesiastes without making a personal judgement on it. Is it the hope, the waiting for something else that transcends its appearance, something new, something other than the repetition of the identical?

All that becomes manifest through the organs of the abyss, of underivable reality, is marked by the constant rhythmic succession of emptiness and fullness, of joy and sorrow. Hiding and showing are intimately bound, pain and pleasure can never be disjointed. Why should we call this rhythm illusory and search for absolute happiness which, as such, is abstract? Indeed Qoheleth invalidates this process by considering it an illusion of existence.

> Why make myself so wise?
> I will gain nothing more from it
> And in my heart I say
> This too is vanity.[32]

The difference between knowledge and ignorance is not denied by Ecclesiastes, yet this does not prevent him from speaking, at least, about the frustration of existence because he encounters nothing new beyond the rhythm of life. But why is he unable to find it? Because he looks for it in the rhythmic appearing of beings. All is 'wind,' therefore nothing can ever assume a fixed shape, it remains forever indefinite and will forever escape rational definition. All is 'wind,' 'breath,' 'gasping': in them, the rhythm and the order of reality make themselves manifest.

The fact that Qoheleth takes as his points of departure the pain and pleasure of beings so that he may then wonder about and identify absolute pain and absolute pleasure, new and beyond the limits of the game of existence, this fact points to the limitedness of his perspective on the problem. In spite of his 'method of the heart' he begins with an abstract conception of beings. His attempt to find something new that will give meaning to the individual being's experience of pain and pleasure, proves to be a dead end; consequently, his pessimism originates in the long wait for the unfeasible. Qoheleth chose the path of pleasure, luxury, power, of everything that makes beings glitter and shine and that

---

[32] *Qoholét o l'Ecclesiaste,* 2:15.

simultaneously casts a dark shadow on their sorrowful transience.

All this means that we base our search on the individual beings themselves and we derive, on the basis of their transience, a negative judgement on existence. Scholars have asked the following question: Does all this searching constitute a negative evaluation of the Hebrew tradition, which presupposes the discovery of a new reality in the realm of a revelation outside of history?

In his commentary on the *Book of Ecclesiastes*, Aarre Lauha points out that the Hebrew conception of originary reality implies a correspondence between man's interior landscape and an ethical order.[33] Misfortunes and defeats always bear witness to a certain awareness. The concept of merit is alien to the Hebrew tradition, and it is precisely this concept that Qoheleth negates in order to deduce from it his fundamental pessimism. Wisdom and ignorance, life and death follow one another in cycles. The order of events is indifferent to the ethics of man. Qoheleth's negative arguments are based, on the one hand, on the lost illusion of finding something beyond existence and, on the other, on the concept of utility.

The domain of usefulness is the domain of beings: exchange among beings leads to usefulness. If we remain in the realm of originary reality, in the realm of oneness, we have nothing to gain and nothing to lose. In that realm there are neither advantages nor disadvantages. In the realm of being considerations of usefulness or uselessness have no meaning. All that exists here is the question of *parousía*.

Where in the text can we find the signs of the originary problematic we are confronted with? We must avoid any misunderstanding about it: such a problematic is threefold. First of all, the pessimism of Ecclesiastes stems from his awareness of the impossibility of going beyond the rhythm of pain and pleasure and beyond the tragedy of existence. Our first purpose in considering the text of *Ecclesiastes* was to show that throughout the history of Western thought, already at its origins in the Hebrew tradition with Qoheleth's teaching, we detect the awareness that by starting with the question of individual beings we cannot come to the understanding of being as such which will therefore remain forever a mystery.

---

[33] Aarre Lauha, *Kohelet. Biblischer Kommentar Altes Testament*, vol. 19 (Neukirchen-Vluyn: Neukirchener Verlag, 1978).

In the introduction to his commentary on the *Book of Ecclesiastes*, Lauha stresses right at the onset that the text should be interpreted as a protest of the soul against the dogmatic and theological conception of Jewish scholastic wisdom. Qoheleth's reflections on existential reality invalidate the theory of the self-realization of justice. The axiom behind the idea of a reward for ethical action is thus proven untenable: "The awareness of the indifference of history with respect to an ethical order, caused Qoheleth to doubt and inevitably led him to challenge traditional beliefs."[34] Elsewhere Lauha states: "Qoheleth's God is not the God of the Jewish faith: for him man's relationship with God is different from the one found in the Old Testament. Qoheleth does not know that God, whom man can address as 'Thou,' and with whom he can carry on a dialogue."[35] God is distant: "God is in heaven and you are on earth."[36] "The faith of the Old Testament presupposes that man can confide in God. Qoheleth does not know it [. . .]. The central dilemma lies in the fact that for Qoheleth the question about the meaning of life cannot be answered on theological premises, but only with the aid of reason—and yet he knows human wisdom is unreliable."[37]

The second essential issue in *Ecclesiastes* is the fact that Qoheleth—though convinced of the failure of traditional faith—does not really break with the spiritual tradition of his people. Although he cannot relate to traditional doctrine, he concedes that a social community can exist only within a moral order: "Even though Qoheleth's image of God is very different from the prevalent one of the Old Testament, it still represents a salutary, necessary warning concerning many important principles of faith [. . .]; his writings remind us of God's sovereignty and transcendence, and constitute a perspective in opposition to any kind of immanentistic religiosity or pantheistic piety."[38]

---

[34] Lauha, 15; also J. Pedersen, "Scepticisme israélite," in *Revue d'histoire et de philosophie religieuses*, 10 (1930), 347 ff; and J. Fichtner, "Die Altorientalische Weisheit in ihrer israelitisch-jüdischen Ausprägung," in *Zeitschrift für die alttestamentliche Wissenschaft*, 62 (1933), 74ff.

[35] E. Pfeiffer, "Die Gottesfurcht im Buche Kohelet," in *Gottes Wort und Gottes Land. Festschrift für H.W. Hertzberg zum 70. Geburtstag*, ed. H. G. Reventlow (Göttingen: Vandenhoeck & Ruprecht, 1965), 158.

[36] *Qohélet o l'Ecclesiaste*, 5:1.

[37] Lauha, 17.

[38] Lauha, 23.

The name of God appears frequently in Qoheleth's text, but his purpose remains hidden:

> A grievous affliction this
> That God has put on man
> To torment him.[39]

> All God's deeds
> He places in men's hearts
> Where they are a reflection of His world.
> But God hides from man
> The purpose and the reason
> Of His doing.[40]

> Be circumspect
> When you go to the house of God
> Approach and listen
> Only evil can come
> From the offerings of fools.[41]

> Observe what God has made
> If He has made it bent
> You cannot straighten it.[42]

> You experience all in God's creation
> Yet of all things existing
> Of all that happens under the sun
> Man cannot discover the meaning.[43]

> You cannot fathom
> God's doing which is all.[44]

The third issue is of utmost importance. One of the interpolators who glossed Qoheleth's text after its redaction, though he is aware of the failure of the Hebrew tradition, does not redeem it with a metaphysical theory but refers himself to the pre-eminence of language, of

[39] *Qohélet o l'Ecclesiaste*, 1:13.
[40] *Qoholét o l'Ecclesiaste*, 3:11.
[41] *Qoholét o l'Ecclesiaste*, 4:17.
[42] *Qoholét o l'Ecclesiaste*, 7:13.
[43] *Qoholét o l'Ecclesiaste*, 8:17.
[44] *Qoholét o l'Ecclesiaste*, 11:5.

the word. Such a word, he concludes, remains 'unheard,' it does not
correspond to the word of the Hebrew tradition.

Qoheleth wanted to find

> The exquisite word
> The precise writing
> For the true word
> Wise man's words
> Are pointed and sharp
> And like nails thrusted in
> Are the writings that contain them.[45]

It is precisely here that the text deals in explicit terms with the
question we tried to confront in the course of our work. It is not
merely a matter of showing, as Ecclesiastes has done, that we cannot
begin with the question of the transience of beings in order to reach
an understanding of being—this is in fact the origin of all pessimism.
It is rather a matter of confronting the very question of being itself,
by identifying it with the impetuousness and the elenctic nature of
the 'exquisite' word, of the word that is 'pointed and sharp,' that
reveals the sign which our author cannot discern in Hebrew theology, as his undeniable pessimism ultimately confirms.

The interpolator concludes: "The word is now silent."[46]

The pessimism of Ecclesiastes is intimately related to the impossibility of going beyond the rhythm of pain and pleasure and consequently of going beyond the tragedy of existence as painfully experienced by Western man, a concept, this, radically different from any
of Zen Buddhism. Buddhist philosophy is grounded on the idea of
the cyclical reappearance of one single reality to which we must grow
accustomed without admitting its tragic aspects.

Qoheleth knows the word of the God of Israel, but he is not
satisfied by it and he therefore criticizes the Jewish tradition. The
interpolator, however, is well aware that Qoheleth sought 'the
exquisite word' and the mysterious, sacred reality it represents in the
abyss of its history. But, in spite of his quest, the exquisite word is
still 'unheard.'

---

[45] *Qoholét o l'Ecclesiaste,* 12:10–11.
[46] *Qoholét o l'Ecclesiaste,* 12:13.